OTSEGO COUNTY IN THE CIVIL WAR

Firsthand Accounts of War Experiences

Compiled by
Otsego County Historical Association
Dominick J. Reisen, Editor

Contributors:

William Beardslee
Nancy Beardslee
Duane Bliss
Anna Buell
Leigh C. Eckmair
Harriett Geywits

Richard Graham
Ronald Jennings
Frank King
David Petri
Sherlee Rathbone
Leslie Rathbun

Virginia Schoradt

SQUARE CIRCLE PRESS
VOORHEESVILLE, NEW YORK

Otsego County in the Civil War:
Firsthand Accounts of War Experiences
Civil War 150th Anniversary Edition

Published by
Square Circle Press LLC
137 Ketcham Road
Voorheesville, NY 12186
www.squarecirclepress.com

©2011, Otsego County Historical Association. All rights reserved. Introduction ©2011, Otsego County Historical Association. Newspaper articles contained in this publication are in the public domain. The private letters, diaries and other remaining content are held in various private or public collections; any person or organization wishing to reproduce content contained herein is required to contact the publisher in writing.

First edition published 2005. Second edition published 2010. Third edition, revised and expanded, published 2011.

Cover design ©2011, Square Circle Press LLC.

Printed and bound in the United States of America on acid-free, durable paper.

ISBN 13: 978-0-9833897-4-3
ISBN 10: 0-9833897-4-8
Library of Congress Control Number: 2011933355

Acknowledgments
The acknowledgments of the Otsego County Historical Association appear at the beginning of this book.

CONTENTS

Acknowledgments, v

Introduction, 3
The Prelude, 8
Enlistment, 26
The War Front and The Home Front, 36
Surrender and Aftermath, 114

Appendix I: Men from Otsego County Selected for the Draft, 129
Appendix II: Medal of Honor Recipients from Otsego County, 144

Bibliography, 147

Index of Authors, 151

ILLUSTRATIONS

Gilbertsville Monument, 24
Morris Monument, 25
Cyrus J. Hardaway, 27
Richfield Springs Monument, 34
Cooperstown Monument, 35
Lansing B. Paine, 76
Andersonville Prison, 107
Oneonta Monument, 112
Worcester Monument, 113
Cherry Valley Monument Re-dedication, 126-7
Cherry Valley Monument, 128

ACKNOWLEDGMENTS

The Otsego County Historical Association (OCHA) would like to extend its sincere gratitude to the many people who made this book possible. Support for this book came in many forms, from just sharing words of encouragement and inquisitive interest, to actually providing physical material. The response from those who were contacted for material was incredibly positive.

Because this project generated such a flood of sincere enthusiasm, it became gratifyingly obvious that by creating a "commemorative token" worthy of the 150th anniversary of the Civil War, OCHA had struck a chord within the Otsego County historical community. We hope this book gives living meaning to the soldiers and their families that endured the hardships and sacrifices during the "war between the states."

Among the many contacts and contributors, Harriett Geywitts is recognized for her dedicated research that brought this publication to maturity. Without her patient and deliberate use of the World Wide Web, some details of the Civil War on the Otsego home front would have gone undiscovered and not made it to these pages.

A special acknowledgment is extended to the Exeter Historical Association for sharing material.

The support of Wayne Wright, Jo-Anne Van Vranken, and Evan Rallis at the New York State Historical Association Library was invaluable.

Without the committed efforts of OCHA Board Member and editor, Dominick Reisen, Town of Middlefield, this publication would not have come to fruition. Other members of the 2010–2011 OCHA Board also played a significant role in getting this book to publication. The support of Les Rathbun, Town of Middlefield, Sherlee Rathbone, Town of Otsego, and Virginia Schoradt, Town of New Lisbon, was the primary catalyst for making this happen.

Finally, OCHA extends its grateful appreciation to Richard Vang of Square Circle Press for his patience and guidance in getting this material into a finished format that can be read and enjoyed by all.

Anna M. Buell, President

OTSEGO COUNTY IN THE CIVIL WAR

The story of valor is written,–
How they marched, how they fought and they bled
How few there came back without blemish,
And the many they left with the dead.

John K. Tyler, Company G
Born in Westford

INTRODUCTION

The Civil War was perhaps the most pivotal event in the course of American history. The Revolutionary War and the equally revolutionary peace settlement created a society with the highest and most noble ideals; primary among these were those sentiments expressed in the Declaration of Independence that "all men are created equal." This was a sentiment born out of the Enlightenment, of which many our Founding Fathers were children. America became unique in this period as a Western society in which sovereignty and governmental authority sprang from the people generally, rather than from a singular person, a monarch. Looking back from the present vantage point, when this idea has gained primacy, it is sometimes hard to grasp the radical nature of this proposition. Although it is fair to say that the idea of popular sovereignty was qualified in the United States until the twentieth century, when finally all adults could vote, the basic premise had gone unchallenged since the founding. The Founding Fathers had defined "the people" as adult male property owners. Over time the property qualifications lessened and "adult male" expanded until property was no longer a qualification and "adult male" became simply adult.

Along with this radical notion of popular sovereignty, the founders also created a political settlement based on the idea that semi-sovereign states could band together in a loose federation. These states would form a united federation of states, but would retain many of the characteristics which defined independent sovereign units. This concept first took form in the Articles of Confederation. Later, in 1787, a constitution was written which, although giving more power to a national government than the prior system under the Articles had, was still easily interpreted as continuing to hold the idea of state sovereignty as being paramount.

Throughout the first half of the nineteenth century both of these ideals were repeatedly tested. The ideal of the equality of man was contrasted with the stark reality of slavery and human bondage. Immediately following the American Revolution, several northern states took up the question of slavery and commenced its slow abolition, sometimes painfully slow. The abolition of slavery and the slave trade within the British Empire in 1807 coupled with its slow abolition in the northern states of the Union only highlighted the abomination that was slavery in the southern states. Living in the warm glow of the Enlightenment, most people felt secure in the idea that slavery would slowly wear itself out in the south, and they only need show the southern states the example of living without slavery for these states to bring themselves to abolish slavery. Indeed, on Jubilee Day, July 4, 1827, when slavery ended in New York State, Hayden Watters of Middlefield, when addressing a crowd at the Presbyterian Meeting House in Cooperstown, stated that "his coloured brethren" now needed to practice "sobriety, honesty, and industry, together with a proper regard to the education of their children." The stress was on living a productive life and thereby setting an example for others including those of the south who maintained that two races could not live together.

This idea of "moral suasion," as it was called, that is, setting an example for the south proved ineffective in ending slavery where it continued to exist. In fact , many who advocated the merits of slavery, sought to expand it further into the fresh lands of the west. By the 1830's the abolitionist movement began to turn to more militant tactics. Going into the southern states and denouncing slavery, peppering the south with abolitionist literature, assisting slaves to escape their masters infuriated slave owners while at the same time causing abolitionists to rally around various political ideas and parties that sought to end the westward march of slavery. An uneasy co-existence developed between the states which periodically erupted into open confrontation.

The strength of the abolitionist movement within the northern states, and indeed the English speaking countries in general, led the southern states to re-examine that second ideal laid out with the revolutionary settlement: that the United States comprised sovereign states within a federal Union. This concept was challenged during the first Nullification Crisis of 1822 and then the second Nullification Crisis of 1833, when South Carolina maintained that it, and indeed any state, had a constitutional right to declare any federal law void within its boundaries if that federal law was contrary to state law. The logic of the proponents of Nullification rested on the notion that since the states were equal parties, along with the federal government, to the Constitution by virtue of their initial adoption of the Constitution, they, therefore, had a right to opt out of it, or any piece of the federal governmental structure they deemed incompatible with their states' laws. If this was the nature of the states "contract" with the federal government, then there was an inherent right of individual states to declare certain federal laws as contradictory to state laws and therefore, null and void within a given state. Those opposing Nullification held the contrary view, that once a state adopted the Constitution that state became subject to the federal government and all laws passed by that federal government without exception.

Ultimately, federalism was challenged by the idea that if these states were truly sovereign, if the Nullifiers were triumphant and states could disregard certain federal laws, then states had the right to secede from the Union. Secession meant ending a state's adherence to the federal Constitution and leaving that federal union which the Founding Fathers had established. Here, again, the opposing argument held that once a state adopted the federal Constitution, there was no ability of that state to leave the Union. The theory of secession became reality in the winter of 1860-61, after Lincoln was elected president by a northern-based Republican party. Secession sparked the conflagration that was the Civil War: the war for the preservation of the Union.

When the southern states began leaving the Union in what has become known as the Secessionist Winter, the primary question became: Could the south legally secede. After his inauguration, Lincoln made his position clear: States did not have a right to secede. From this position, the aim of the Union Army was clear. The north was fighting only for the preservation of the Union. Although some abolitionists hoped that this war could be turned to further their cause, that was not the principal aim nor was it the understanding of the vast majority of men who enlisted in the early days. As some of the following letters make clear, these men were enlisting in the Union Army to preserve the Union, not to free any slaves. As the war dragged on, though, and as the men of the army saw slavery as it existed, ideas changed. The Lincoln Administration wrestled with the "slave question" and "emancipation" as a policy concern, but the men in the field slowly became more and more abolitionist minded as they saw how the south had been ruined by slavery. By January of 1862 Elijah Keith of Milford wrote his wife "that slavery is an unmitigated curse." As so often happens, initial war aims changed, in the case of the Civil War, those aims moved from being the preservation of the Union to also being a war to end slavery.

The causes and course of the Civil War are familiar to all students of American history. To attempt a re-telling of those events here is not the point of this book. Instead, what is attempted is a glimpse of the Civil War through the eyes of those men and women from Otsego

County who lived through it. Using newspaper articles, diaries, memoirs and letters, we have sought to give an impression of the war from a first-hand perspective. What did the men in the field think and feel, and what did those left behind think and feel? At times these people felt the weight of their duty in preserving the Union, at other times there was simply the basic instinct of self-preservation driving them. These people spoke of the initial euphoria of war, which turned to hatred at its horrors. Even years after the war ended some men still held bitter feelings toward the south. Reading through Lewis Bryant's experience as a prisoner at Andersonville Prison, one sees clearly his bitterness years after he returned home to Butternuts. As the remembrance of those horrors faded, though, most of these people looked back at the nobility of their sacrifice. War is not always noble, despite the nobility of its stated purpose. The Civil War was no different. Abraham Lincoln gave voice to those noble aims of the Civil War in his Gettysburg Address, stating, "… that from these honored dead we take increased devotion to that cause for which they gave the last full measure of devotion—that we here highly resolve that these dead shall not have died in vain—that this nation, under God, shall have a new birth of freedom—and that government of the people, by the people, for the people, shall not perish from the earth."

These individuals give us a perspective of the war from its varying viewpoints. It is hoped that this book will give the reader a new and perhaps broader view of what the Civil War meant to those who fought it, both at home and in the field. It may seem contradictory to think that the reader can achieve a newer and broader view of the Civil War by reading these first hand accounts which come exclusively from the men and women of one New York county. However, many of the documents in this book have never been published before and through these letters we learn not only of the travails of life on the battle field, but we also see what concerns these soldiers had regarding the life they hoped to go back to at home. Further, because so many of these men knew each other before enlisting, they spoke in these letters about each other to their loved ones at homes as the friends they were. The breadth and nuance achieved here comes from the very nature of taking a selection of first-hand accounts from a relatively small geographic area.

These first-hand glimpses are organized to follow both a chronological and thematic format. The chapter headings give a sense of the content of each section. The first chapter shows the reader how the national debate over slavery and abolition played out in its limited way in Otsego County, beginning with Jubilee Day in 1824, through the bombardment and surrender of Fort Sumter, to the issues attendant to convincing men to enlist. The book ends with accounts of the surrender of the Confederate forces and gives of glimpse of how the remembrance of the horrors of the war merged with and then were overtaken by the sense of the nobility of the cause and sacrifice. Finally, ending with the re-dedication of the Civil War monument in Cherry Valley by the Abner Doubleday Civil War Roundtable, marking the 150th Anniversary of the commencement of the Civil War.

Some of the men who wrote these letters were quite educated, some hardly at all; this led to variations in spelling of common words as well as names of people and places. Within the letters themselves we have corrected some spelling and punctuation when modern usage dictated minor changes; when those changes would necessitate a major re-write of the document, original construction and spelling has been retained (without the use of *sic* to indicate original misspellings). In the interest of consistency and space, dates of letters, when included in the greeting header, have been removed and placed in the article title. Hyphenation was not employed. Where necessary for contextual clarification, words in [brackets] have been inserted, or a note added under the article heading.

The Civil War was indeed a pivotal event in American history. The men who fought this war made great sacrifices, many, approximately 620,000, made the ultimate sacrifice. Whether they realized it or not, their sacrifices ensured the perpetuation of those ideas which our Founding Fathers wrote into our society: all men are created equal and the United States is a federation of states. Their sacrifices also led to the ending of slavery on the north American continent and ended the notion that states could legally secede from the Union. In many ways these men gave us the pluralistic and more tolerant society in which we take pride. For all of these reasons, they should be remembered and their words should live on.

Dominick J. Reisen, Editor

THE PRELUDE

Excerpt from *The Freeman's Journal,* July 9, 1827

Connected with the events of the Fourth, the celebration of the day by the *Coloured people*, as the one fixed upon by Statute for the abolition of *Slavery* in this State, ought not to pass unnoticed. They met, to the number of about sixty, and marched to the Presbyterian Meeting-House, with music and their banner flying, where an Address was delivered by *Hayden Watters*, stamped throughout with much good sense and correct observation of the character and habits of his coloured brethren. Curiosity had led rather a large assemblage of white citizens to be auditors of so novel a scene, and we venture to say, that not one of them left the church without having been gratified with the very appropriate matter furnished by the speaker. His advice, if practiced, would prove a blessing to the African race, as it inculcated the necessity of sobriety, honesty, and industry, together with a proper regard to the education of their children. Every thing was conducted decently and in order.

Excerpt from *The Freeman's Journal,* September 7, 1835

PUBLIC MEETING

The undersigned, citizens of Otsego County, feeling that the measures pursued by the advocates of the immediate abolition of Slavery, are prejudicial to the peace and quiet of the American Union, and tend directly to a dissolution of the Confederacy of the States composing it deem it important that an expression of public sentiment should be had upon the subject in the County; and, to that end, they respectfully request the attendance of their fellow citizens generally, without distinction of political party or religious sect, at a public meeting to be held at the Universalist Meeting House, in the Village of Cooperstown, on TUESDAY, the 15th of September, instant, at 2 o'clock in the afternoon. Dated Sept. 1, 1835.

Excerpt from *The Freeman's Journal,* April 9, 1838

ANTI-SLAVERY DISCUSSION

A discussion upon the merits of the Anti-Slavery or Abolition movements which at present so deeply agitate the whole Union, transpired at the Court House in this village on Friday Evening and Saturday, the 30th and 31st ult., and on Monday, the 2d inst. It terminated Monday evening.

We were not present on Friday evening, but are informed the lecture was upon the following propositions: 1st, That slavery is a moral and political evil; 2d, That we [this community] are bound to exercise our political power, to the extent of its constitutional limit, to effect its immediate abolition.

On Saturday morning, after a sort of random discussion, during which some reasons were offered by the mover why the resolutions should pass, separate motions were made, under which both resolutions were laid on the table, and the meeting adjourned *sine die.*

Notice was thereupon give that Mr. [Gerrit] Smith would lecture upon the same subject, in the afternoon, which he did, and likewise in the evening. - J. Fenimore Cooper, esq. submitted a few brief remarks at the afternoon session.

Excerpt from *The Freeman's Journal,* June 9, 1854

A FUGITIVE!

We are informed that a Negro lately made his appearance at Westford, in the county, who represented himself as a "fugitive slave," who had made his escape from his master in Virginia. One day last week, there officers arrived there with the intention of arresting the said "fugitive" on a charge of breaking open and robbing a store, in some other section of country. But certain sympathizing people of Westford – who thought these officers only humbugging, and were desirous of carrying off the "slave" under false pretences – determined to cheat the Fugitive Slave Law out of a "victim;" so they "rescued" the darkey, gave him ten or fifteen dollars, and started him for Canada! We tell the story as 'twas told to us.

The following paragraph from the Utica Observer of Monday last, doubtless refers to the same "fugitive," above mentioned:-

Arrest of an Escaped Burglar

Officer Milo G. Barber, last Saturday morning, arrested a colored man by the name of Warren Victor, who is charged with having committed and extensive burglary in Elmira. Victor was arrested a short time since, but managed to escape the hands of the law, on the 31st ult. A reward of $100 was offered, to which officer Barber is entitled.

Excerpt from *The Cherry Valley Gazette*, April 11, 1860

The Creed of the Parties

The difference in the creed of the various political parties relates mainly to the question of slavery, and the following we believe to be a concise and fair statement of their positions.

The Democrats

That portion of the democratic party known as "Administration Democrats" believe that under the Dred Scott decision of the United States Supreme Court, slavery exists as a national institution in the territories; that the constitutional guarantees and protects it and that neither Congress nor the inhabitants of a territory, have the right to prohibit it.

The "Anti-Lecompton Democrats," of whom Senator Douglas is the leader, believe that Congress has no right to prohibit slavery in the territories, but that the people of a territory have the right to establish or abolish it as they please.

The Republicans

hold that Congress has supreme authority in the territories, and can and ought to prohibit slavery there; while they recognize the right of every State to establish or abolish slavery as its people shall decide, and avow their determination not to interfere with slavery in the State where it exists. Their doctrine is, that slavery is sectional, not national. That is, that the constitution leaves it to the States to settle each for itself; but that it does not establish or carry it into the territories; and that under the constitution, it can only exist by positive State legislation.

The Opposition Party

By this name is designated, particularly in the Southern States, the opponents of the administration. In the South, it embraces the old Whigs and Americans; in some parts of the North, it has embraced Whigs, Americans, Anti-Lecompton Democrats, and Republicans.

The Union Party

The Union Party sprang out of the excitement attending the John Brown affair. It is, perhaps, identical with the "Opposition," only it does not embrace any portion of the Republican strength. Its, object, so far as avowed, is the conservation of the Union.

Letter from Abner Doubleday to Ulysses Doubleday September 23, 1860

Band of North America
Wall Street
New York City

            Fort Moultrie, Charleston S. C.

Dear Brother

 I will not write to you at present in the way I proposed for I doubt if there will be any necessity for it. A little piece of information was obtained here yesterday, which throws a new light upon the state of affairs here. I have all along been puzzled by the way the people, or rather the leaders of the peoples talk. Secession with every one I meet seems to be a foregone conclusion. They all say as a matter of course they must have the forts if they secede, and yet they do not appear to think of attacking us. They deny all intention of doing so, and no appeals are made to popular passions with reference to this place, which would be made if they really designed to take the forts with a strong hand. I think now I have obtained the key to this mystery Trescott is Asst. Sec of State, and before his late visit to this place was acting as Sec. That is, as one of the cabinet. Being a secessionist and a leader, besides being deeply interested as a resident of the sea-board, he would be likely to ascertain the intentions of Government if any man could. Trescott stated unreservedly in his late visit here that there would be no fighting, that the administration would withdraw the troops in the harbor and give up the Forts to the south if secession took place, but that they would put a revenue cutter or a war vessel of some kind to cruise off the mouth of the harbor to prevent any exit or entrance, and would declare Charleston not a port of entry. In addition to these, all postal and telegraphic arrangements would cease.

I do not believe the Administration have the right to give up one foot of U. S. soil to the State of S. Carolina. Castle Pinckney not only commands Charleston, but the interior passage between Charleston and Savannah.

The conversation alluded to above took place between Trescott and Col. Gardner. Col. G. has now adopted some food plans of defence in case of an attack, but they require us to have ample time for preparation and due notice which is not likely to be given.

Ordering Engineers here to put these Forts in complete order at the expense of the U. S. and then turning them over in that condition to S. C. looks rather queer.

Acknowledge the receipt of my letters alphabetically.

There is a great quantity of broken bone fever about, but we have escaped so far.

With love and regards to all

Your aff. brother

Abner Doubleday

Excerpt from *The Cherry Valley Gazette*, April 10, 1861

War Impending
The Naval Force Under Orders.
Fort Pickens to be Reinforced.
A Battle Probable.
Special Despatch to the N. Y. Evening Post

Washington, April 4

The Cabinet in again in session to-day. -The wildest rumors are flying about. Among them is one to the effect that the Commissioners from Montgomery have presented a new communication to the President, peremptorily demanding the immediate evacuation of Fort Sumter and Pickens.

It is now positively known that orders have been sent to all naval stations for every vessel in the navy to be put in readiness for instant service.

Second Despatch

Washington, April 4

The Administration has decided to reinforce Fort Pickens at all hazards. This determination has not yet been officially announced, but there is reason to believe that active measures will be taken at once for the relief of Lieut. Slemmer's command.

Another Despatch

Lieutenant Gilman has just arrived here from Fort Pickens.

He reports that a fight is likely to occur at that point at any moment.

The troops of the Confederate States are concentrating at Pensacola, under command of General Braxton Bragg, and preparations are making for a decisive movement - Bragg is constantly drilling his forces, and has nearly four thousand men under arms. Lieut. Slemmer, however, is fully prepared for the worst. If he is attacked he will give a good account of himself.

Further Warlike Rumors

The Gulf squadron is to be commanded by Capt. Stringham. The reasons for the increase of the Naval forces in that quarter are conjectured.

The extreme caution which characterizes the Administration on this, as well as other military subjects, occasions many warlike rumors.

The Government seems to have come to the determination, in the language of a Cabinet officer, "to be known only by its acts."

Extreme solicitude is everywhere manifested relative to the movements concerning Forts Pickens and Sumter. The fear is expressed that collision may be precipitated.

The steamer Pawnee, now lying off the Washington Navy Yard, will probably leave for ports unknown on Saturday.

Information has been received here stating that Lieut. Talbot left Charleston to-day with important dispatches for Washington.

Excerpt from *The Cherry Valley Gazette*, April 10, 1861

BOMBARDMENT OF FORT SUMTER
THE FORT RETURNS THE CANNONADE

Charleston, April 12

The ball has opened - War is inaugurated. The batteries of Sullivan's Island, Morris Island, and other points, were opened on Fort Sumter at 4 o'clock this morning. Fort Sumter has returned the fire and a brisk cannonading has been kept up.

FURTHER PARTICULARS

New York, April 12

The *Herald's* special despatch says - Moultrie began bombardment with two guns, of which Anderson replied with three shots from his barbette guns after which the batteries as Mount Pleasant, Cumming's Point and the Floating Battery opened a brisk fire of shot and shell. Anderson replied only at long intervals, until between 7 and 8 o'clock, when he opened from two tier of guns looking towards Moultrie and Steven's battery, but at 8 o'clock failed to produce serious effect.

During the greater part of the fray Anderson directed his shot principally against Moultrie, the Stevens and Floating Battery and Fort Johnson they being the only ones operating against him. Fifteen or eighteen shot struck Floating Battery without effect.

It is reported that the Harriet Lane received a shot through her wheel-house - She is in the offing. No other government ships are in sight.

Troops are pouring into the city by thousands and business is entirely suspended.

The answer to General Beauregard's demand by Major Anderson, was that he would surrender when his supplies were exhausted, that is, if he is not reinforced. - Of nineteen batteries in position, only seven have opened fire on Fort Sumter. The remainder are held in reserve for the expected fleet.

THE GOVERNMENT PLAN FOR THE RELIEF OF FORT SUMTER
EXTENSIVE PREPARATIONS
SPECIAL DESPATCH TO THE N. Y. EVENING POST

Washington, 10th. - It is now certain that the government is fully determined to reinforce Major Anderson's command at all hazards. I learn on competent authority that the plan adopted for the relief of Fort Sumter is substantially as follows: In case of necessity supplies are to be thrown into Fort Sumter by means of a number of small boats, which presenting smaller and more scattered marks for the cannon of the rebels will perhaps save an unnecessary bloodshed. The government has chartered a number of small schooners and other crafts which have been filled with sand-bags. that these form past of the Charleston expedition is probable from the fact that the charter does not bind them to go further south than Savannah.

The schooners filled with sand bags will sail in bearing boats on the side which is towards Fort Sumter. These boats will, of course, be entirely protected from the guns of the rebels by the wall like sides and solid contents of the larger vessels. This plan will be adopted only in the event that the Charlestonians fire upon the small steamer loaded with provisions, which will first be sent in. In that case, of course, the fort will receive not only provisions but men, and the plan above detailed is an admirable one by which to throw any requisite force into the fort without probability of serious loss.

Excerpt from *The Cherry Valley Gazette*, April 10, 1861

Latest News
Surrender of Ft. Sumter
The Confederate Flag Replaces the Stars and Stripes
The Barracks on Fire
Explosion of the Magazine
An Invading Army of 75,000
President's Proclamation

Charleston, 13th, via Augusta Ga.

Fort Sumter has surrendered. The Confederate flag floats over its walls. None of the garrison of Confederate troops are hurt.

Gen. Beauregard, with two aids, has left for Fort Sumter. Three fire companies from Charleston are now on their way to Sumter to quell the fire before it reaches the magazines.

Fort Sumter has unconditionally surrendered. The news has just come.

Ex-Senator Chestnut, Ex-Governor Manning, and Mr. Porcher Miles have just landed and marched to Gov. Pickens' residence followed by a dense crowd, wild with joy. It is reported that ten men of Fort Sumter are killed and the Federal flag was shot away by the Palmetto guards at Morris Island. In all 2,000 shots have been fired. No Carolinians hurt. Major Anderson and his men, under guard, were conveyed to Morris Island. Bells are ringing out a merry peal and people are engaged in every demonstration of joy. It is estimated that there are 9,000 men under arms on the Islands and in the neighborhood.

Major Anderson has reached the city and is the guest of General Beauregard. Our people sympathize with Major Anderson, but abhor those who were in the steamer off the bay and in sight of our people, and did not even attempt to reinforce him.

Excerpt from *The Freeman's Journal*, May 3, 1861

A subscription is being circulated in this village [Cooperstown] to aid in the formation of a Military company, the services of which will be tendered to the Governor. It has been suggested that when the subscription reaches the desired sum, the subscribers to the fund should be called together for consultation and the appointment of a committee to act in concert with the officers of the company. If we have those among us who desire to enlist under the Stars and Stripes at this time, the citizens of Cooperstown will not be backward in subscribing aid toward the support of their families during their absence. This is being done in every city and village that sends forth a company. The State authorities furnish arms, uniforms and equipments to all whose services are accepted, and their pay commences from the day they commence drilling.

Excerpt from *The Freeman's Journal*, May 10, 1861

A Military Soiree will be given at the Eagle Hotel this [Thursday] evening, by citizens of this place, complimentary to the Officers of the Fifth Division. S. S. Burnside, General. Music by Crumwell's full band.

A number of our citizens meet three of four times a week at Burgess Hall, for military drill. They will be ready to respond to the call of the Government for troops, when needed.

It has been proposed to organize a "Home Guard" for

Cooperstown, with the understanding that it shall not be required to leave this village unless invaded.

Excerpt from *The Freeman's Journal*, May 17, 1861

The meeting at this village on Thursday and Friday of last week, of most of the Generals and Field Officers of the 5th Division, left a very favorable impression with our citizens as to the character and general bearing of the gentlemen holding these offices. The Division embraces portions of 11 counties, and includes four brigades and eight regiments. Considering the imperfections of the present militia system of this State, the 5th Division is in good condition, and will compare favorably with any in the interior of the State. The officers made a fine appearance in their full-dress parade on Friday morning.

The Soiree, on Thursday evening, was well attended, and was a very pleasant affair in all respects. The following has been handed in for publication: -

A Card: -

> At the meeting of the officers of the 5th Division N. Y. S. M., held at Cooperstown on the 10th inst., the following resolution was unanimously adopted. In behalf of Major General S. S. Burnside and Staff, and Brigade and Field Officers of the Division, as a testimonial of regard for kindness, hospitality and attention given them by the Ladies and Citizens of the Village of Cooperstown, we offer the following resolution: -
>
> Resolved,
>
> That we tender our regards to the Ladies and Citizens of this village for the kind attention, and for the tasty, polite and bountiful manner in which we were treated at their "Soiree" last evening.

Letter from
J. Lafayette Rider to Mrs. Lyman Foote of Cooperstown
(published in *The Freeman's Journal*, June 21, 1861)

New York, June 17, 1861

Madam:-

As the recipients of a supply of Havelocks sent by the "Women of the village of Cooperstown," through the kind favor of the Union Defence Committee, we embrace this, the earliest moment of expressing our profound gratitude to those ladies for the opportune favor thus derived through their patriotic efforts in a common cause, and desire to assure them that while we will be greatly benefited by having our heads kept cool for action, our hearts have already been warmed by this evidence of interest in the comfort and happiness of the volunteers, on the part of the women of Cooperstown

Respectfully yours, J. Lafayette Rider, Colonel

Excerpt from *The Freeman's Journal*, August 16, 1861

The ladies of this village interested in raising money and making up articles for the sick and wounded soldiers, confine their efforts to the Volunteers from their own State - of whom there are over forty thousand in the field. They co-operate with the Army and the Women's "Central Relief Association," having their head-quarters in New York City, at the head of which is Dr. Mott.

Notwithstanding the liberal provision made by Government for the sick and wounded, the volunteer aid received through this Association and from other sources, has been very grateful to the recipients. There are now about 950 reported in the hospitals in and near Washington. The female nurses, employed for the first time in the Army, have rendered very efficient service - aided and sustained as they have been by the Relief Association alluded to above.

Otsego is not to be altogether unrepresented on the battle field. Within the past few weeks quite a number of army recruits have been obtained in this county. On Wednesday morning about 40 men left this village to form a company in the Van Guard Rifle Regiment. They were mostly from Milford, Laurens and Fly Creek. They are to go immediately into camp on Staten Island. Recruits will be received for this company, during the next two weeks at the Otsego Hotel.

Excerpt from *The Freeman's Journal,* August 30, 1861

Capt. H. W. Lyon, of New York, is recruiting a company in this county for the Ira Harris Cavalry; recruiting offices, Tryon House, Cherry Valley and Otsego Hotel, Cooperstown. The pay in this arm of the service is $15 a month for privates. Horses and all equipment furnished by the Government.

Excerpt from *The Freeman's Journal,* October 4, 1861

The desire that this county should be represented on the battle-field for the Union, by a regiment of her hardy and intelligent yeomanry has been often expressed, but yet, with about 300 men enlisted, we cannot, that we are aware, point to a single company as entirely our own. Our men are scattered about in various regiments and companies, in squads of from five to thirty men, Thus Otsego receives little or no credit for what she has done to uphold the Government in this contest.

It is now thought that, with perhaps some aid from our neighbors of Chenango and Delaware, a Regiment may be speedily formed, and a camp of instruction organized at this place. Hon. R. Franchot, Member of Congress for this District, having conferred with the State authorities and received assurances of all necessary aid and encouragement from them, has issued the following appeal in hand-bill form.

A Camp of instruction at Cooperstown. Whenever eight Companies of thirty-two men each, shall be raised from the counties of Delaware, Otsego and Chenango, an order will be issued from the Adjutant General's office for a Camp of Instruction at Cooperstown. The Volunteers will be furnished with subsistence, arms, clothing and camp equipment, as soon as mustered into service.

I am encouraged to believe that within ten days time, the required number of men to organize a regiment can be mustered at Cooperstown, and in common with all loyal citizens, I trust that a combined effort may be made to effect this object.

Have not the citizens of these three Counties, pride of locality sufficient to place themselves on a par with other Counties of the State? Let the hearty response of every loyal man to this invitation, prove this confidence is not misplaced! I pledge myself that all the provision above enumerated, will be carried out by the proper authorities.

R. Franchot

Mr. Franchot informs us that several gentlemen have already assured him that they can and will raise companies for the "Otsego Regiment," to command which competent officers can be obtained without any difficulty.

The citizens of Cooperstown, we are confident, will extend a helping hand in this laudable effort. The Fair Grounds could be converted into a convenient Camp; tents, &c., will be furnished by the State.

At a meeting of those interested in this movement, held on Wednesday evening, the following gentlemen were appointed a Central Executive Committee: F. M. Rotch and L. J. Walworth, Otsego; Samuel F. Miller, Delaware; and Adrian Foote, Chenango.

It was resolved that the members of the Executive Committee in each county be authorized to appoint a sub-committee in each town of their respective counties, to further the patriotic object in view.

Excerpt from *The Freeman's Journal*, October 11, 1861

Col. Shaul's Regiment, the 39th, have voted to go to war under him, and efforts are being made to fill up the requisite number. The encampment will be at Cherry Valley. In order to aid in this movement, no further steps will be taken to open an encampment at this place. The 39th will be known as the "Otsego Regiment," and we hope its ranks may soon be filled.

Excerpt from *The Freeman's Journal*, January 17, 1862

We are requested by the Committee having in charge the receiving and forwarding of articles for the benefit of our Soldiers in the hospitals, to state that a second box will be sent during the ensuing week.

Those persons who have taken yarn for the purpose of knitting, will please send in such completed work as soon as possible, as the season is now far advanced when such articles are most needed.

Further contributions are solicited from the liberally and charitably inclined. Materials for drawers and comfortables, if sent immediately, will be made up and forwarded. Let not our energies slacken, demand will be urgent and never ceasing while the war lasts.

Excerpt from *The Freeman's Journal*, February 14, 1862

Doubleday's Band, of this village, having been hired by the N. Y. 66th Regiment, left this place for Alexandria - where the Regiment is stationed - on Monday Last. The Band comprised the following members: L. M. Doubleday, leader; Wm. H. Doubleday, S. H. Bingham, Thos. H. Bingham, Sam B. Lewis, Chas. J. Tuttle, of Cooperstown, Warren Beardsley and James Beardsley, of Cherry Valley and Senaca Duel of Mohawk.

The 66th will have good music, and the Band, we hope, will have a good time and a safe return at the close of the war.

Excerpt from *The Freeman's Journal*, July 11, 1862

Volunteers are Needed to reinforce our brace army in the field. How shall they be obtained fast enough, and in sufficient numbers? The Government offers liberal pay; but the inducement is not sufficient in this crisis. Men are needed now, and they must be had, or the rebellion becomes a success.

Otsego County should furnish 400 of the 50,000 men New York is called upon to raise. To do this promptly, she should donate $50 to each volunteer, as an additional inducement to enlist, or to assist in taking care of his family. Why should not the country, as well as the cities, aid in this manner? Let the Supervisors of Otsego County meet immediately, and vote to raise $20,000 by loan to aid in this movement. The amount must be paid in four years, and none of us feel the poorer. Shall it be done?

Excerpt from *The Freeman's Journal*, July 25, 1862

The Committee appointed for the town of Otsego had a preliminary meeting on Tuesday evening - E. M. Harris, Chairman, and J. Worthington, Secretary. It was not the deemed best to designate any of the officers for the company proposed to be raised in this town, but the following resolution was adopted, and those wishing to volunteer, can enroll their names at either of the places designated:-

Resolved, That Marcus Field, John Worthington and J. B. Hooker, of this town are designated to receive the names of persons who may wish to enlist in the Regiment to be raised in this Senate District: and those desire to join the Company to be raised in town, are requested to leave their names with either of the above named gentlemen.

The Committee desire to call attention to the following inducement to volunteers, so far as pay is concerned:- Bounty to Volunteers.

The compensation now offered to volunteers is of the most liberal character. The private receives his regular pay of $13 per month, $100 bounty from the General Government, and those from this State will now receive a special bounty of $50 under the arrangement just decided upon by Gov. Morgan. Besides this, $2 is given every volunteer. This goes to the volunteer if he enlists of his own accord. This makes the aggregate pay of a private, as follows, per year:-

Regular monthly pay	$157
Government bounty	$100
Special State bounty	$50
Enlistment pay	$2
	$309

In addition to clothes and ration, each man receives $25.97 monthly wages. In all human probability, the Rebellion will be crushed out, and the war concluded within a year. There are few men, comparatively, that can secure a better income in any other way.

A Grand War Meeting is called at this place, on Wednesday next. Let the meeting be largely attended by the patriotic and loyal men of Old Otsego. Hundreds of her gallant sons are in the field. They need reinforcements. Shall they have them?

Excerpt from *The Freeman's Journal*, August 8, 1862

At a meeting of the taxable inhabitants of the town of Otsego, held pursuant to call, at the Court House in the village of Cooperstown, on the 6th of August 1862, Wm. H. Averell, Esq., was elected Chairman and M. B. Angell, Secretary. E. M. Harris, Esq., Chairman Town Military Committee, offered the following resolution, -

> Resolved, That the Supervisor of the town of Otsego be authorized to borrow on the credit of the town, a sum sufficient to pay each volunteer, resident of the town of Otsego, already

enlisted or who shall enlist, under General Order No. 52, pursuant to the call of the President of the United States for 300,000 volunteers, twenty-five dollars, in addition to that paid by the General Government and the State; one-half to be paid when accepted and mustered in at the Regimental depot, the residue to be paid when they are accepted and mustered into the service of the United States - to the number of at least 50 men, and that the same be levied and assessed upon said town.

On motion of E. P. Byram, J. P. Sill, J. R. Worthington and J. H. Story were appointed a committee to co-operate with the Supervisor in negotiating a loan, for the purpose of paying a bounty of $25 to each volunteer resident of the town of Otsego, pursuant to call of order No. 52 and the resolution adopted above.

This mode of raising a town bounty is the only equitable one - and it seems to meet the hearty acquiescence of all tax-payers. The aggregate bounty, to resident volunteers of this town, now amounts to $175.

Excerpt from *The Freeman's Journal*, October 31, 1862

For most of the town in this County there will probably be drafted into the army men on whose labor women and children are depending for their support. The soldier can not send home more than $5 to $10 a month of his pay; he needs some of it for his own comfort. He may not receive his pay promptly. His family must not be allowed to suffer during his absence.

We call upon the benevolent and patriotic men in the several towns in the County to look to this matter and to organize some system which shall not have the families of absent soldiers dependent on chance or charity. They must have our watchcare and aid, wherever needed. The soldier who is poor, and who is drafted into the service, must leave his home free from care on this subject.

Gilbertsville Monument

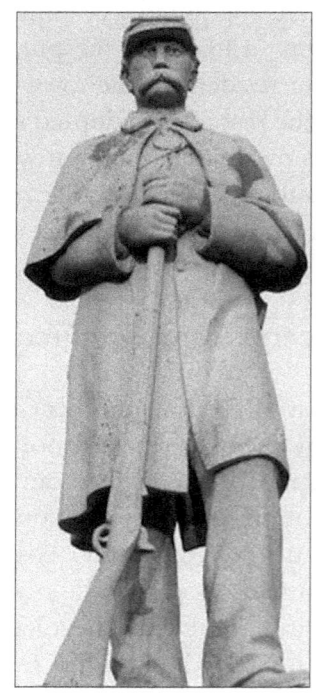

Morris Monument

N.Y.
CHARLES L. KENYON U.S.N.
 Died Aug. 7 AD 1866
WILLIAM D. ADAMS 8 REG'T CAV.
 Killed at Beverly Ford Va. June 1863
WALLACE W. JACKSON 114 REG'T
 Killed at Winchester Va.
IRA A. DAVIS 114 REG'T
 Died at New Orleans
ALEXIS GOODRICH 179 REG'T
 Killed
AARON A. PARCELL 176 REG'T
 Died at New Orleans
WILLIAM E. GREENE 21 REG'T
 Died in Salisbury Prison
JOHN S. SCUDDER 20 REG'T
 Died at Prison at Bowl. Va. 1864
JAY BANCROFT 121 REG'T
 Killed at Spotsylvania May 1864

LIEUT. GEORGE YODER
DAVID H. LEWIS
CHAUNCEY KELSEY 152 REG'T
SAMUEL G. PARCELL
ALVIN KINNEY 152 REG'T
DANIEL MILLER
LEVI MCINTYRE
HENRY STOCKWELL
RICHARD BENNETT

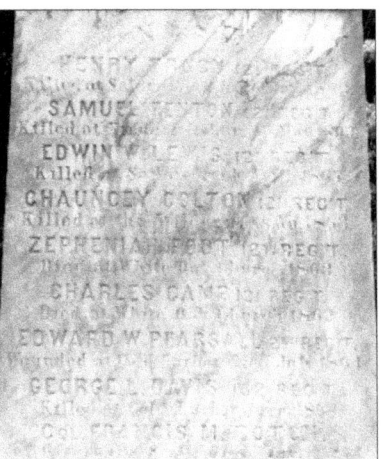

HENRY
 Died at S
SAMUEL
 Killed at
EDWIN
 Killed at
CHAUNCEY COLTON 152 REG'T
 Killed
ZEPHENIAH 121 REG'T
CHARLES CASE 121 REG'T
EDWARD W. PEARSALL
GEORGE L. DAVIS
COL. FRANCIS H.

APPLEGARD
STANLEY SHERCART
ADELBERT ELDRED
GEORGE
HENRY ROGERS 8 REG'T
WILLRED
JAMES

ENLISTMENT

Excerpt from "War Reminiscences" by Delevan Bates (published in *The Otsego Republican,* October 25, 1895)

In the summer of 1861 a war meeting was held in the little village of Westford, in Otsego County. Some young men residing on the hills of the adjacent town of Worcester, from idle curiosity attended this meeting. Among the speakers was Lieut. Allen. His words were full of patriotic devotion to our country and ended by pledging his life to maintain the integrity of the Union. In one short year his pledge was redeemed and his life's blood was spilled on southern soil. Another lieutenant in the 51st N. Y. Vols was William H. Leonard of Worcester, who afterward became a surgeon in the regiment. He was a brother of Doctor George Leonard of East Worcester, who was one of the principal physicians in that part of the country for many years preceding the war.

Excerpt from *The Cherry Valley Gazette,* January 15, 1861

Departure of the Otsego Regiment

The volunteers at this depot, numbering 500 men, left here for Albany last Wednesday. There were five companies, commanded by Captains Swan, Young, Cook, Hansen, and Bowdish. As early as nine o'clock, the streets were crowded by fathers, mothers, sisters, brothers, and friends of the volunteers and before ten o'clock, one hundred and four teams had been provided for transportation to Canajoharie by the farmers hereabouts. But about seventy-five of them, however needed. At about 11 o'clock the line was formed and after marching up as far as Story's hotel, the sleighs were filled and started for Canajoharie, a mile and a half from where they were met by two brass bands and a large crowd of people, and escorted to the depot. A few regiments of picked men, such as the Ellsworth and Sharpshooters, have probably a better class of soldiers, but we doubt whether a nobler and more hardy body have left any portion of this State. The ladies of our village and vicinity were engaged much of the time while they were here, manufacturing mittens and other articles of comfort not furnished by government, and most of the men were provided with such articles. The many idle and absurd rumors about the misconduct of the volunteers while here, were without a particle of foundation, and were fabricated by parties who desired to prevent enlistment. A better behaved set of men we have never seen, and we cheerfully bear witness to the falsity of such slanderous imputations. They have gone forth to do battle for their country; not an act was done while here which would cause a single mother to blush for the deeds of her son, and we doubt not that those who return will be able to point to an honorable and spotless career. A few of the sick still remain here, under charge of Lieut. Rob't Story.

Letter from Cyrus J. Hardaway of Pittsfield to his Mother December 27, 1861

Albany

Dear Mother

Last night was my first of genuine soldier life We got in Albany at two o'clock PM. And I looked the capitol over and then went to barracks which was the worst thing that I have seen yet. Had frank and beans for supper and each man had to go to the shed and fill his own tick with straw and then march back to the barracks and make up the beds. All we had to do was lay the ticks down and then put the blanket over us and the bed was done. There is about 1500 soldiers in the barracks now of all sorts I slept in a room with about 250 last night Expect to leave tomorrow sometime. The picture that I sent home was for Libbie. Have not been homesick any yet and hope that I shant be. I shall let you know where to write as soon as I can find out myself. Please sent me the Freemans Journal as soon as you can find out where to send it

Your aff son, C. J. Hardaway
Sternbrix Hall

Cyrus Hardaway (right), and his friend St. John

Letter from John Harkin of New Berlin to Maria Harkin
January 26, 1862

Camp Riker Island
76th Regt. Camp H.

Mrs Harkin, Madam

I wish to inform you where I have been since I left New Berlin Jan 8th. We encamped in Albany until the 18th when we went to New York and staid until the 21st when we went to Riker Island 10 miles from New York. It is an island situated in the Sea the ocean surrounds it on all sides. It [is] a cold dreary place in winter the Baracks is very cold the rain and cold comes in through every seam.

I do not know how long we will be here. When we left Albany they said we were going to Florida. We may not be here but a few days and we may be here a week I cannot tell how long. There are a good [amount] of sickness here all from colds. Lewis Blackman, Charlie Davis, George Bosworth, Edwin Waters all of our company have been in hospital.

This is the 2d letter I have sent and have recvd no answer. I wrote you before I left Albany. We get up at 5 o'clock in the morning and the lights are all put out at 9 P. M.

There are no good water here as it is all salt water. They make the coffee in salt water but I do not take any of it, it makes the Boys all sick.

We do not drill but very little here as the weather is so very cold. The breeze [off the] beach is very cold. There are plenty of clams and oysters here.

I have nothing of importance to write at present. I send my love to all the children to Susan Waldo, Libe, Lewis, Charley and Alice. Tell them to be good children let me know if Waldo is got well. Let me know if George had written yet. If he has let me know where he is or send me the directions.

I have a very hard cold ever since I came here but it is a general complaint here as there are 100 men in the one apartment and I have to write this on my knee and now having no more to say at present but hoping to find you all in good health I bid you all good bye.

John Harkin

    Direct you letter Care of Capt A. L. Swan Commanding Co. H 76th Regt NYV, Riker Island NY
    Better observe the directions

Letter from Thomas F. Weldon to James Weldon
February 3, 1862

Philadelphia

Dear Brother Jimie

I suppose you began to think you would never hear from me well I will tell you how things went with me we left Albany five O'clock the next Friday after I wrote home arrived in the city the next morning then stopped at the Park Baricks three days each day expecting our pay we than went up the East river to Rikers Island

I waited for my pay before I would write so as to send it home the paymaster finely come and paid us off I drew 36 Dollars we were all paid to the first of January the day before I left the island I had writen a letter to Send you but that night the Col came from the city with news that the next morning, last Friday, we had to Start for Washington So that I had no chance to mail my letter

Well the morning we started all was hurry and bustle in camp emptying ticks Boxing Blankets and etc. so that by ten o'clock we were in line ready for to march well we marched down to the pier got aboard the boat went forty miles up the east river to amboy we took the cars there for the land of Dixie got to Philadelphia about twelve O'clock at night the ladies of the city had Supper all ready for us at the Cooper Shop hospital the Hospital is sustained by the laides and citezins of the city for Benefit of the Sick and wounded Soldiers to and from the seat of war well our regt went on to Washington and as I had a Bad cold my Capt told me to Stay to the Hospital while I got beter I have got over my cold now as I have been here 3 days and I think that by the after tomorrow I will Join my Regt

The night Before last there were twenty of the Wounded Prisoners from Richmond the Dr came in the Same night and dressed there wounds Some had their limbs crushed By shells others a rifle ball through one of his lungs out in his back but still he lived and was geting along well

I think tomorrow I will go to Join my Regt So you need not answer this until you hear from me again I am going up this afternoon to Sharps Rifle Shop and to the Navy yard they are to work night and day casting canon and Balls Shells etc the wether is warm and pleasant about as it is with us in the State first of April the city is a Beautiful one the streets are as regular Just like a checker board well I have not time to Write eny more at present Enclosed you will find thirty Dolars which is all I can Spare at present as we Only drew pay to the first of

Jan So that in a few days pay Day will come around again no more at present

Yours truly, Thomas Weldon

Excerpt from *The Freeman's Journal*, July 25, 1862

Young Men of Otsego
to Arms!
The New Regiment

To be raised in Herkimer and Otsego, should be one of the first in the field. You are therefore invited to come forward promptly and enlist.

A company is being raised by officers who have Recruiting Stations in Cooperstown, Cherry Valley and Springfield Centre. It will be the first company of the regiment, and have the post of honor.

Pay $13 to $23 a month, commencing on the day of enlistment. $27 bounty paid by the United States when mustered into service. (Men to be mustered into service a week after enlistment, or sooner.)

FIFTY DOLLARS BOUNTY paid by the State of New York, when mustered into service. $75 bounty paid at the end of the war - making the entire bounty $152

The Cooperstown Office is in the building adjoining the Journal Office on the west.

Douglas Campbell, Recruiting Officer
Cooperstown, July 23, 1862

Excerpt from *Experiences and Activities of a Lifetime* by Henry Hilton Wood of Middlefield

Politics ran high and father took a great deal of interest in the questions of the times, leading up to the Civil War. In 1862 I was growing tall and strong, so I was hired out to work for Mr. Ogden Beach, in Springfield Township, beginning the first of April, and remained until the 8th of August. I had not lost a day from work or spent one dollar of my wages. Father and my brothers James and John came to see me and wanted me to enlist, as Lincoln's second call for 300,000 more volunteers had been issued. They thought it would be better for the three of us to go together. I went home with them and on the 12th day of August, 1862, we three brothers enlisted in Co. E. 121st Regiment Volunteer Infantry of New York.

The next day we left home for the camp where the regiment was forming at Herkimer in the Mohawk Valley, about twenty-two miles from home. The morning we left was a very trying time. It was hard to say "goodbye" to father, mother, brother, sisters, friends and the old home that had become very dear to me. We walked three miles to Cooperstown, then a large wagon, drawn by four horses, loaded with recruits, with flags and streamers flying, started on the journey to the camp. There were several other wagons just like the one we were in. Along the road people were gathered in throngs, waving flags, cheering us and wishing us "God-Speed." We arrived at camp late in the afternoon and were immediately examined for fitness for service. The examination was thorough, and some were rejected. My brothers and myself were accepted. We were then taken into a large mess hall for dinner. We were hungry, as we had had nothing to eat since early morning. We were then shown our tent, a large one, eight of us to sleep in it. Straw was put on the ground for our bed, no clean "nightie" like we had at home, one blanket for each. In the morning we went down to the canal to wash, as the dust and dirt of the previous day was still on our hands and faces, no towels; hardships of a soldier's life had begun. We were then sworn into the United States service. Regulations were read to us. At the end of each one was "Death or such other punishment as a Court Martial may direct," for disobeying. We then began to realize what we were up against.

Excerpt from *The Otsego Republican*, August 30, 1862

Notes of a Trip to Camp Schuyler

Camp Schuyler, so called from Fort Schuyler, of revolutionary fame is located on the banks of the [Mohawk] river, about a mile and a half from Mohawk village. As we approached the encampment we found ourselves in the midst of a throng of people going and returning, and presently saw the guards walking to and fro, marking the division line between the crowd without and within. Passes are easily obtained by those who have friends to visit among the soldiers and we soon found ourselves in the city of tents, exchanging kindly greetings with the brave Otsego boys, who have taken their lives in their hands, and pledged them for the maintenance of our blood-bought institutions.

Col. Franchot wants only experience to be acquired by actual service to make him every inch a Colonel; his fine figure is set off to advantage by the military uniform, and his bearing is calculated to inspire his men with confidence in his ability to command, and with a desire to discharge faithfully their duty as citizen soldiers. Lieut. Col. Clark has seen service as a Captain in the 43d regiment of New York volunteers, which was so badly cut up before Richmond that only enough men for five companies survived. Maj. Olcott, favorably known to many citizens of this county, also passed through hard fighting on the Peninsula, where he was brevetted for his bravery, first as an orderly and then as a Lieutenant, and then as Captain. Adjutant Ferguson has not seen service, but is familiar with the duties of his office, did competent to discharge them. Capt. Galpin, and Capt. Wendell, and some of the Lieutenants of the regiment have also seen service and the Captains and Lieutenants, and the non-commissioned officers, with very few exceptions inspire one with confidence that they will fill their places with credit. The regiment is well officered, and as we looked at the men, we could not but feel that they were of the bone and sinew of Otsego and Herkimer, and far superior to the class of men who have heretofore enlisted. They were sustained by a mingled spirit of determination which will carry them creditably through the fight, and of good humor which will bear hardship patiently, and keep disease at arm's length. It may safely be predicted that the 121st regiment of New York Volunteers, after a few week's drilling shall have given them the requisite discipline will not be excelled in physical or moral force by any regiment in the field.

Excerpt from *The Freeman's Journal*, December 25, 1863

The Town Meeting called for the 23d inst., assembled at the Court House and organized by the appointment of Rev. Martin Marvin, Chairman and Samuel A. Bowen, Secretary.

The object of the meeting was stated to be raising of a bounty to pay Volunteers. The reading of an Act of the last legislature, forbidding the paying of local bounties, was called for.

L. I. Burditt, Esq., took the ground that the town should not act directly against the law - which was adopted for the wise purpose of preventing a competition between different localities - but that we should await the further action of the legislature. E. Countryman, Esq., said there was no doubt that the legislature would repeal the Act of last year, and legalize the action of this meeting.

Mr. G. L. Bowne moved that the town pay a bounty of $500. Mr. Countryman moved $600. The amendment was adopted.

The following resolutions, on behalf of Mr. C., were adopted:

> Resolved, That the sum of Six Hundred Dollars shall be paid to any and every person who shall hereafter volunteer as a soldier in the army of the United States, from the town of Otsego, to be allowed on the quota of said town under the recent call for volunteers by the President of the United States, the same to be paid whenever said volunteer shall be accepted and mustered into the national service.
>
> Resolved, That bounty money be raised by assessment and taxation on the taxable property of said town of Otsego, in the same manner that town taxes are levied and collected by law.

The following were appointed a committee to superintend the raising and paying out the money; H. H. Hooker, Dr. Lathrop, E. Countryman, Fayette Hinds, John B. Hooker.

The meeting then adjourned.

Martin Marvin, Chairman

Samuel A. Bowen, Secretary

Excerpt from *The Freeman's Journal*, January 8, 1864

An adjourned town meeting was held at the Court House in this village on Monday last. Scarcely one hundred of the tax payers of the town were present; very few, especially, of the business men of Cooperstown were there. H. Sturges, Esq., was appointed Chairman and A. Bowen, Esq., Secretary

The committee appointed at a former meeting made a report, to the effect that they had obtained sufficient signatures to notes making them good for any reasonable amount; that none of the capitalists or banking institutions of this town would advance the money on them; that a number of men had already enlisted, expecting to receive a town bounty of $600; that they had information to the effect that several veterans now in the Army had been enlisted to the credit of the town of Otsego; many new men were ready to enlist; the committee had done the best they could to carry out the wishes of the former meeting, and they now asked to be discharged. One of the committee further stated that some of the volunteers were ready to take the bonds of the town.

Mr. Hendryx moved that the proper town officers be instructed to issue town bonds, to the amount of $600 to each man willing to enlist and take the town bounty in that form.

This motion appeared to meet with very general favor - especially among the tax payers present - and it was, after some discussion as to details, passed; the bonds are to be for $200 each, and to have one, two and three years to run - so that the tax for this specific purpose will be about $14,000 each year.

Mr. Shaw moved that the Committee be instructed to favor the Veteran volunteers mentioned in their report, in preference to all others, so far as possible. Carried. The quota of the town of Otsego is nearly or quite made out; there may be one of two lacking. Eleven veterans from the 43d Regiment re-enlisted and desired to be credited to this town. We were last evening shown a letter from C. Bowen, Esq., dated at the camp of the 3d N. Y. Cavalry, Newbern, in which he stated that 15 men of that regiment had re-enlisted and desired to be credited to this town, or to some other town in Otsego. He said, "I could fill up your entire quota from this regiment."

Richfield Springs Monument

Cooperstown Monument

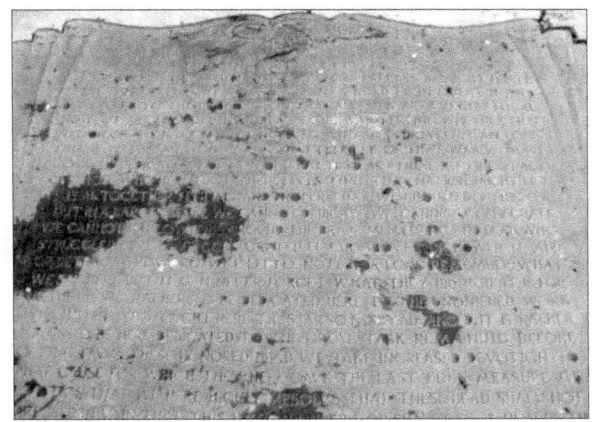

THE WAR FRONT AND THE HOME FRONT

Letter from Amasa Cook Myrick of Gilbertsville to his Father December 2, 1861

Fort Worth

Dear Father,

    I received your letter today but there is not much in it. I wish when you write you would tell me what is going on there. There is the devil to pay amongst the boys here and the people at Gilbertsville. Some of the boys receive letters every day stating that some of the boys write home that our Quartermaster Henry Bushnell and Orderly Sergeant Charles A. Hurlbult have connived together to cheat us out of our rations and pocket the money, and today he received a letter that he had been trying to cheat us out of our pay which is all utterly false and very unjust and we have heard that some of our boys have been writing home that this is so. And if this is so I wish you would try and find out who it is. It would oblige us very much, for find out we will if it costs us a journey home and back again. I have heard that I wrote home to you that we had been two days without anything to eat and what we did get was not fit to eat. If this is the case I wish you to write to me and tell me the same and I will have it read before the company and if they wish to tar and feather me they can do so and I will find out about this matter and let me know as soon as possible. We hear rumors every day about the boys that some devilry is amongst us and that we do not like very well.

    I can write to you no news of any consequence except within a week there has about 20 thousand troops encamped within half a mile of us and there is about 14 or 16 thousand more coming here this week. We can raise an army of 200 thousand men within 2 hours ride. I wish you would send me a lot of postage stamps. Send me about fifty for we can not get them because we can not get passes to go where they are and they hate to take the change or money for fear that letters may not reach home.

Please to ask Mr. Green what regiment Isaac is in and the captain's name and what company he is in and if he is near us. I will try to find him. Tomorrow I am going to see Henry Smith. Please write as soon as you get this.

Yours truly,
Cook Myrick

>Direct to:
>Fort Worth Alexandria, Virginia, 2 Regt. N. Y. V. Artillery Co. E care Capt. Klinck. Please put on these directions.
>I can not tell you where our flying artillery is for I have not seen it myself.
>Please not to sell any of my clothes. If it did not cost you to much I should send home for a pair of boots with legs that comes up to my nees made of kipskin. If you would send me a pair get some that are double soled and he has go the measure of my foot. Get Leland Parks to make them, be sure and not get them to small. They will cost about 5 or 6 dollars and I can not get them here short of 10 or 11 dollars. Our shoes are poor miserable things and will not last more than 2 months. I have got to have some more within 8 [?] weeks at the utmost. I wish you would send me the boots if you can possibly. Our payday comes next January and then I will send you some money.
>Cook Myrick

>Perhaps you think I have spent all money but I have not yet.

Excerpt from a Letter from John Phinney, written on his behalf by Dwight Reed
Camp of Instruction, Washington, DC, January 1862

John says he is going to send some money home as soon as he gets well and perhaps it will not come further than Cherry Valley, where, he says you had better inquire. He would like to have you write what kind of horse you have, also what hops are bringing. Enclosed you will find some leaves that were picked at the White house a few days ago. Our camp is about one mile and a half north east of the capitol on a low rim brow, which we have a fine view of the city and the Potomac beyond.

In the two regiments there are about fifteen hundred men, fully one company having died. Privates are not allowed to go outside of the lines without a pass, so we are having rather a dry time here just now. We have not got our rifles yet, but Col. Berdan says they will be here in twenty days . The rebels will perhaps have a chance to taste a little cold lead, allowing that we get sight of them. There is prospect of a big fight before long as there are indications of an advance movement of our troops. John and Ed Marks were sent on parole last Thursday night. They were about one hundred rods apart. John says the only thing he saw was a fox which he ordered to halt but it did not stop.

If John's health does not improve you may expect a letter again shortly.

He sends respects to inquiring friends, and I guess he would like to send love to some one but I do not know.

Hoping that you will write soon. I close.

Yours affectionated,

John Phinney

Per Dwight Reed

Letter from George Snow of Cherry Valley to John Bocock January [?] 19, 1862

Washington

friend John

Robert Story has got back and told me that he has Seen you and you and him took a big drink together he told me that you had Sent me a box of Stuf from home i Was glad to here it but We are A going to move tomorrow and i dont now as i can in Joy it as must as i Could here i will get it to day and it will Come good to eat on the road

we have had a big time here for the last week we got our pay and all had a drunk i for one was down to the Sity fore days and three nites you bet i tore things got drunk and Sober and drunk a gain but got back Safe a gain

i Sent forty dolars to Chery Valley by express to Charls McClane for you i Want you to go and get it and pay William hall What i ow him and John Danals what i ow him and the rest keep for me give mother as fore dalars too by her a new dres and the rest keep till call for by mother

we have marching orders and we espect to go tomorow We may not go till Wensday i dont now where we will go for Shure they to

Forteres monrow but i dont think it be futher then virginy but i dont now mor close whare i is as long as i keep new

i am corpral of the gard to day and hant much time to rite now So must Close

So good by from George Snow to John Bocock Direct your leters as before

Excerpt from a Letter from Elijah Keith of Milford to his wife, Caroline
January 12, 1862

The storm is over now and we have as fine a day as you ever see in June, warm and pleasant and I think this is justly called the sunny south for we have most all pleasant weather tho the nights are cold I think if slavery had not ruined this country it might have been one of the best states in the union but as is, no northern man can fail to see the contrast that exists between this and the free states and if I had come here a friend to slavery I should now be an abolitionist. What little intercourse I have had with the people here convinces me that slavery is an unmitigated curse, considered in any light, either physically mentally or morally; politically or religiously, or pecuniarily; for according to common reasoning a man compelled to labour without promise of reward cannot be expected to do as he otherwise would and the master expecting gain or profits from the unrequited labour of another must in the very nature of the case fail to accomplish the desired object and religiously considered who but a fanatic would for a moment believe that a man could be guilty of the foul robbery, the sum of all villany, and still claim the name of Christian, it has managed to muffle most of the pulpits in this country and wherever it exists that is according to accounts I have had and only a partial one sided gospel is permitted in the presence of the Negroes and I hear the whites have so long listened to it that they are left to believe a lie that they may be damned and politically considered it has debased many wise men and drawn them into a laboured defence of the system and the name abolitionist is a name more dreaded by many than that of traitor or rebel and many of our laws have been enacted and executed with an eye to its extension and perpetuity and I consider the politics of the country to some extent poisoned by the curse and our country must get rid of it morally considered it is an institution that draws around it every immorality known to the moral world and mentally and physically, body and mind goes down together under the weight of the blighting curse, master and both sink under its degrading influence.

You must go around and visit the friends just as if I were there and try to enjoy life and keep up good spirits and if I ever come home I shall know how to prize the society of home and friends.

Letter from Cyrus J. Hardaway of Pittsfield to his Mother February 2, 1862

Washington

Dear Mother

It is once more Sunday with everybody but soldiers with them there is no difference in the days with exception of having a little more to do Sunday than any other day in the week. First comes a regimental inspection after that the companys are drawn up in line in front of the tents for inspection of knapsacks blankets tents etc. everything has to be just so, if things are not put up right the boys have to take a blowing up. I have escaped blowing so far as my bump of order is rather prominent You wish to know if I go to Church any. I have not been to Church since I have been here because I have not had a chance with the exception of going to hear Cheever in the house of representatives. I suppose by the way you write that you hear a great deal about the Sharp Shooters. There is a great deal in the papers about them. Some of it is true but the great part is what is commonly called lies the Colonel has persevered he has got an order for the Sharps Rifles and we shall get them about the first of March and that will be as soon as we shall want them. Since we have found out that we are to wait here we have laid out twenty five dollars in fixing up our tent. It is built up about six feet with boards and banked up with dirt and then the tent is put right on top so that is makes a very nice house. We have built bunks and have got good straw beds and plenty of blankets so we can sleep just as well as though we were at home. We have a man that does cooking for the whole company it is all done at the kitchen so all we have to do is eat and grow fat Since pay day we have dry toast butter and coffee every morning for breakfast. I have not seen Ed in some time but hear that he is getting along I went through the Smithsonian Institute last Thursday and saw a great many curious things among the best was a piece of meteoric matter that was found in Mexico weight 232lbs I think if that had hit a man on the head when it fell he would have heard something drop. The next time that I go to town I shall go through the

Navy Yard I suppose that there is as much to be seen there as any other place in town. Washington of itself is a most miserable town that I ever saw. If the public buildings were not here it would not amount to more than Peck Town. Your letter are just about right, you might make them a little longer if you have time. Tell summers that I will answer his letter pretty soon I sent home a paper the other day that I got from Fred Barnum

You aff son
C J H

Letter from Cyrus J. Hardaway of Pittsfield to his Mother February 9, 1862

Washington

Dear Mother

I had begun to think that I should not get any letter this week but yours came just in time to save the week. I have been out since dress parade looking around the country and also through Glenwood Cemetery which is the most beautiful place I ever saw. The Country around Washington is splendid. I think if I live through the war I shall make my home in the south for you know that I have always had a great desire to do so. The past week has been quite an exciting one in our camp. Last Sunday night after everybody had gone to sleep the Captain came into our tent very still and wanted ten good men and chose me as one of them so up we jumped and dressed as quick as possible in the dark for we were not allowed to light a candle. We were then marched up to the Colonels quarters where we found that each company had turned out ten men each making in all eighty men. After we were formed in line each man received a Colts revolving rifle with five charges in them and all ready cocked for action we began to think by this time that something was going to be did. The Colonel then gave us orders to fire when he gave the command and be shure and take good aim. We then marched down to the second Regt and arrested three officers and most of a company but did not meet with any resistance as we expected we then marched up to the officers mess tent and had to stay there all night and four times since but have to sleep on our arms every night without taking off boors or any thing else. I guess we shall not have to do it much longer for the mutiny has pretty much died out. I can not describe my feelings exactly the first time that I went out but I think I felt a little worry for I did not know what I was going into. The second regiment have taken Colts revolving rifles and will probably be ordered off in a few days. Our regiment will get Sharps rifles about the first of March and then away we go. Some say to Missouri and some say to Texas but we can tell better after we get started. I will send home some photographs as soon as I can. I am glad you have sent some butter for we can't get good butter here all the time and we have to pay twenty five cents. We frowned at that. The boys go out foraging once in a while and milk all the cows they happen to find so we have bread and milk once or twice a week. You say that you lay awake with the blues on account of the war. I should advise you not to do it any more. I am a great deal nearer to it than you and I assure you that it does not keep me awake a minute. I have not had a letter from Lib yet think she is not very punctual, but as long as I don't get my letters I shan't have them to answer there is some consolation in that. Tell Somers I will send him some papers and answer his letter right away. As it is time for roll call I must Say good night.

You aff Son
C. J. H.

Letter from
Charles W. Devoe of Springfield to James and Delia Devoe
February 17, 1862

Camp Casey, Washington D.C.
Head quarters of the 76th Regt

Father and Mother,

To night finds me as well as common and enjoying myself as well as any one can be expected to do. There is great doings in camp to night. There has been a great victory somewhere but we did not get direct reports but the morning papers will bring the news correct. The report is that there has been 1500 rebels taken prisoners.

Yesterday there was a call made for volunteers to go out on a gunboat expedition somewhere and no one knew where. There was to be one out of each company. There was but three in our company myself and another young fellow from Springfield and a Dutchman and the dutchman was the lucky man to go.

I should have writen yesterday but I was on picket duty and I had no time to write then. You spoke about that money that I was going to send home you said you expected it before this time. The reason that I did not send it right away was that I did not want to send it in a letter and I could not get to a banking house to deposit it, so I took it my head to take care of it in a new way. So I sent to New York and got the whole amount in boots and sent them along a head of us and I have sold them all except two pair. I am not making any thing on them but will save my money. As soon as I get my next pay I will send it all home so that you can have it by the first of April. You need not fear of my spending it foolishly for I am bound to save it all. It cost us something to rig up our houses so that they are comfortable

I have seen E Stickeny, Shutes, Clyde Ripp and Depuy Quartant and a great many others from diferent parts of the country. Some of our neighbors are leaving us every day this morning the 77th that was in camp close by us went down the Potomac and tomorrow the 87th leaves for nearly the same place. There is some talk that our regt will be disbanded and sent home [after the war is over]. J F Newell is here in our regt. he is well as common. I do not see him very often although his tent is not ten rods from mine. It is some muddy here and the neighbors know enough to stay at home and not track their friends floors.

write as soon as you can and do not give yourself any uneasyness about me yours.

with respect give my love to all Chas. W. Devoe

Letter from Cyrus J. Hardaway of Pittsfield to his Mother March 24, 1862

Fortress Monroe

Dear Mother,

You may think it strange to get a letter dated here We broke camp last Thursday at 2 o'clock pm and marched three miles beyond Alexandria in the rain, poured right down all this afternoon and it was not very pleasant marching. We have to lay out in the rain that night Friday at 4 o'clock we started for the boars and made out to get on board about 10 o'clock at night. There is some twenty or thirty thousand troops in the fleet and among them are the 14th Col McLamartin and the Ellsworth Regiment. We came down the river on one of the Hudson River boats. There is quite a number of them here, it was a splendid sight to see the fleet coming down the river. There was no less then twenty steamers in sight all the while and with the flags flying and bands playing it made rather a gay scene. The Captains of the Albany boats had a number of races yesterday which made rather exciting times. We are laying now between Fortress Monroe and Sewalls Point Can see the Stars and Stripes on one side and the Palmetto flag on the other. The gun boat Monitor that the paper have said so much about is lying but a short distance from out boat, it looks like a long platform with a large cask setting on top of it that is the best description that I can give of it. We are attached to Gen. Porters division which is said to be the best lot of troops in the Army. I can not tell where we are going too Some think to Richmond and some to help Burnside. I do not care much which it is if we only come out at the top of the fight. We have been living on Sea biscuits since last Tuesday I have had only one Cup of Coffee since we started from Camp. If you write to me you will direct your letter to Washington just the same as you have done all the time. I have not time to write any more at present.

    Your aff Son,
    CJH

Letter from
John E. Hetherington of Cherry Valley to Lt. Col. Trapp
Camp near Falmouth, Virginia
March 31, 1862

Col.

    I have the honor to respectfully request leave of absence for 10 days for the following reason.

    I left home nearly one and one half years ago, expecting to return in a few months at the farthest leaving business in the hands of a partner and as things have shaped themselves it becomes <u>very</u> necessary that I should visit home this spring.

    It will be of great advantage to me pecuniarially.

    I also wish to procure a uniform.

    Very Respectfully

    John E. Hetherington

Excerpt from
"A Visit to McClelland's Army" by Harvey Baker
(in *Oneonta in Olden Times and Bits of Oneonta History*)

During our tramp this day [during March 1862] we passed a large field entirely covered with the carcasses of horses. Their number must have been many hundreds. What was singular was that none of them had sufficiently decomposed to emit any odor. We entered many of the rebel forts. No civilians had yet appeared upon these deserted army grounds except our party, and the five personal friends of President Lincoln ... who had come on a pass obtained directly from him.

After leaving Holdens and Bull Run we returned through public roads, army roads and across battle fields to the Red Mills and the Orange & Alexandria railroad track back to Fairfax station, as tired a lot of men as one would wish to be or see. On our way we wished to enquire the route to a certain military road which had been constructed for our army, and I entered a house for such purpose. A person was covered in bed, head and all, pretending to be sick. In answer to my inquiry a man trying to assume a woman's voice directed me to the next house for the information desired. Amused at the incident for a man's voice had bade me "come in" when I knocked at the door.

At the next house a woman stood in the door as we approached it. I made the inquiry and received the desired direction, as the road was then within our sight. Seeing no one around I said to her "You are not living here alone, are you?" Her answer was "All are off to the war. There is not a man in the neighborhood."

At that moment I saw a man going from the house to the barn at the next farm not thirty rods away. When some eight or ten rods from the house we had just left, I happened to look back and a man was standing beside the woman in the door looking us over as we were walking cross-lots towards the military road.

On arriving at the road I found an Irishman living in a log house at its side. I commenced talking with him and found him communicative. He assured us that we were running a risk as the people were rebel, and advised to get within the army lines as soon as possible.

Soon after leaving him we heard two rifle reports in the woods only a short distance from us. The next day we learned that two Union soldiers had been shot.

While in Centerville [Virginia] Mr. Dibble and myself were anxious to obtain each a confederate shinplaster [currency] of small denomination.

The two daughters of Dr. Alexander had a number of them but they would not sell them for silver or gold. Determined not to be disappointed in obtaining them, we started next morning for the largest farm house within sight feeling confident we could find some there. On arriving no person was found except an old Negro wench well advanced in years.

She assured us that she was the only person left on the plantation and that her mistress had gone south and her master with the rebel army and that all the slaves except herself had left the plantation.

Mr. Dibble inquired of her, "Well, Aunt Dinah, what do you think of the war anyway?" Her prompt answer was "I don't care whether Lincoln be president of Jeff Davis be president, old Dinah hab to work for a living anyhow."

Upon inquiring for shinplasters she brought forth two half-dollar ones, both old and worn, which she was willing to exchange for bright silver of like denominational value.

Excerpt from
"A Tribute to Eliakim R. Ford, Long Oneonta's Most Distinguished Citizen (Part 2)" by Harvey Baker, (in *Oneonta in Olden Times and Bits of Oneonta History*)

Early in March in 1862 Dr. S. H. Case, E. R. Ford, Cornelius Miller, David Dibble and myself went to Washington to see the army, our children and friends and to learn what we could of the great rebellion and the future outlook. We arrived in the city the first day after the Monitor so signally triumphed over the famous iron clad Merrimac.

In the afternoon Mr. Ford and myself decided to visit the government navy yard at the mouth of the Charles river, and entered a bus for that destination. Seated beside me was a former law partner of Secretary Stanton. Mr. Ford was seated directly opposite to us. The conversation naturally turned upon the success of the Monitor and its possible future use in the war. From that it drifted to other naval ships. I described to him somewhat in detail the form of a steam ram which I thought would stave in the hull of any wooden ship then afloat. I also described how the same ram could be made to overturn any ordinary sized ship.

He said to me "I want you to go with me this evening to Secretary Stanton, and say to him just what you have said to me." Mr. Ford immediately said to him with much decision "that would be impossible, for we start for home this evening." The bus had just then arrived at the navy yard and we parted and I did not see my friend again.

It had been understood that we were to take the next morning train instead of the evening train and I did not know as the arrangement had been changed. Being busy looking over the government works I made no inquiry why our time of departure had been changed. After leaving the ship yard we returned by way of the capital to bid good bye to kin and other friends after getting our suppers and settling the bill we took the evening train for New York.

An hour or so after we started Mr. Ford came to my seat and asked Mr. Dibble, who was with me, to change for a while to his, which he did. Mr. Ford then said to me, "I came to explain to you the reason of our leaving Washington to-night instead of to morrow morning. I listened to all you said to ------- and if you had gone with him to Secretary Stanton and repeated what you said to him, you would have been retained to superintend the immediate construction of the ram, and then what would have become of our poor railroad?"

Letter from
Charles W. Devoe of Springfield to James and Delia Devoe
March 30, 1862

Fort Mass, Washington D.C.
Head quarters of the 76th Regt

Father and Mother

It is with pleasure that I take my pen to write you a few words. I should have writen to you before but I was waiting to get some news to write but cannot get any thing of any importance. The paper do not contain any.

The most news that I have is that a large body of troops have left here to go on the Burnside expedition but I do not know where they are going. 50,000 fifty thousand men that had been in camp within a mile of us left last Thursday. there was the 30th NY and a regiment called the Chauseurs and the 7th and 10th Mass and the 2nd Rhode Island. They only constituted one Brigade. the sharpshooters have gone across the Potomac and we expect to go south in a few days.

We had a review yesterday for the purpose of being attached to Gen Doubledays Brigade. I do not know whether we were accepted or not. We have not got our pay yet but the officers tell us we will get it in a short time. As soon as I get it I will send you some money. The weather is nasti here again. It snowed here last quite fast but now the snow is all gone.

I was on guard night before last and the man that relieved me was shot through the arm. They try to keep it as still as possible. It was about a quarter of a mile from camp and last night they called for Volunteers to take the post. They got six my self among them and about two o'clock I saw a man coming along toward me and I holled him and he snaked a pistol at me but it missed fire and then he started to run. I thought it was my time then so I let him have and wounded him in the leg. It proved to be a man that lives near here. we have him under close guard in our camp.

The weather is bad here yet last night it snowed, and to night we are having a thunder shower. You may send me 50 cents worth of postage stamps next time you write and I will make it right with you. I made out to get a stamp of one of the boys that sent home for them but I must stop now for it is most bedtime. Give my best respects to all the friends in Milford

truly Cha W Devoe

fort Mass Washington D C Company K 76th Regt NY Vol
in care of J W Young

Letter from Cyrus J. Hardaway of Pittsfield to his Mother
April 8, 1862

In Front of Yorktown

Dear Mother,

I received your letter dated the 30th also one from Libbie the same date last night. It did me a great deal of good to get them for I had given up all hopes of getting any letters for sometime to come. We are lying about a mile and a half from Yorktown but do not go into town very often. We started from camp at Hampton last Friday and marched about four miles this side of Big Bethel where we found the first battery. The Sharp Shooters were deployed as skirmishers and marched for the fort to draw fire of their guns. They fired two shots at us and then our batteries opened on them and they left about as quick as possible, they were very strongly fortified then but did not have guns enough to support them against a heavy force the only booty there was a few blankets and two prison boys about 17 years old Genl Porter has one of them for a guide. We camped six miles for Yorktown that night at Cockeltown where we found Sutters Stores six casks of Syrup and fifteen bushels of Peanuts. That was all dealt out to the soldiers that night we had quite a jolly time over it. The Sharp Shooters were started in the morning in the advance of the whole army as scouts and skirmishers, which is not much fun as you do not know what you are going to run into. The first introduction we had was a canon ball whistling over our heads from a fort about a mile from us that we had not heard of. The next was a shell bursting within ten rods of me but did not hurt any one, our Artillery then came up and engaged with them and we went on under cover of our guns we crawled up within 80 rods of their guns and got behind a rail fence and began to fire on them picking off the gunners very fast we succeeded in stoping their fire after about an hours firing. I would not go through the same thing again for the world unless I was obliged to. We were placed right between our cannon and the for so that they both fired exactly over our heads, and those shells make the most horrible noise that I ever heard. I would have given a good deal if I had been at home about that time The Rebels had their Sharp Shooters just the same as ours only they were firing at us and did not trouble our gunners any I got quite used to the whistle of a rifle ball and did not care much about them after I had heard them a while, but I never can get used to the whistle of a shell and hope that I shall not have to take the same position that I had Saturday while I am in the service. The position that we held all day has made lions of the Sharp Shooters but I had rather not be a lion than go through with it again I had quite a compliment paid me yesterday by the Colonel General Porter sent to him for ten of his best shots to go with him on a scouting expedition and the Colonel chose me as one of the ten to go. Professor Lowe is here with his balloon and has been up several times so we have shows here without paying a quarter for it The Rebels are very strong here and there will be a terrible battle before we ever get possession of Yorktown but I think the most of it will be done with artillery for it would be impossible to get them out with the bayonet. They have got 80 or 100 guns within a circle of about three miles and could shell us out of camp now if they wished to but I guess they have not any more ammunition then they want for they will have a hot time in a few days and they are aware of it. They knew of our coming as soon as we started from Washington one of our boys found a letter here telling the names of the Regiments that had started and ours among the rest. We have been camped by the side of the 14th Regiment ever since we came to Fort Monroe and I see all of the New Berlin boys every day. Charley Beardslee sends his love to you and hopes to get back so that he can see you again. The boys in his company say that there is not a better soldier in the Regiment then his is. Remember me to all and write as often as you can but you must not expect to hear from me very often.

Your aff son
CJH

Letter from Cyrus J. Hardaway of Pittsfield to his Mother May 10, 1862

West Point

Dear Mother

I have not heard from you yet but shall continue to write once a week as long as I am able to do so. Time gets away so fast that I can hardly keep track of the weeks to say nothing about the days. There was quite a heavy battle at Williamsburg last Monday, we could hear the guns all day and expected to be called upon all day but did not go, had just got nicely to bed when the order came to fall in for a fight. That means with only haversack and canteen on. It came rather tough for the rain was pouring down in torrents but the regiment has not turned out so many men at one time since we left Washington as it did that night. We were formed in line in five minutes from the time we were called which is called pretty good time for a regiment to get out in. We stood in the rain about fifteen minutes and got pretty well soaked and then we were ordered back to our tents to await orders, did not have to come out again that night and have had a pleasant time since. Spent two days in Yorktown looking things over. I think if the rebels will leave such a place as that is that they can not make a stand any where. We went aboard the boat at dark and in the morning we woke up and found ourselves at West Point. There had been quite a skirmish here a day or two before we got here, and some fifty or sixty of our men killed. They were just burying the dead as we landed. It looks rather hard to see them put in trenches without any coffin but I suppose it is just as well so as any way. I have talked with a number of wounded men that were in the fight and they say that the niggers are the worst men in the rebel army. They cut two or three of our mens throats after they were wounded form ear to ear. The pickets have orders now to shoot every nigger they see outside of the lines. I think the order will be obeyed too the mark. Every man here sweats vengeance on the black devils. When we were lying before Yorktown Porters division had all the word to do because they were in the advance.. Now some other division has taken the head and we are held in reserve for which I am not very sorry. We are encamped now in a large wheat field of about fifty acres. The wheat is about four inches high. It seems to bad to read it down but it has no business to be Secesh. We have had our Sharps rifles nearly a week now. They are the most beautiful piece I ever saw. They are shure of a rebel anytime at half a mile. There is not much more that I can think of to write about now, as soon as I get to Richmond I will write again would like to hear from your before I start.

You aff Son
C J Hardaway

Letter from
Lester K. Winslow of Springfield to Angeline Winslow
May 13, 1862

My Dear Mother

I now sit down to let you now how I git Along I am well at present and hope that these few lines will find you the same this is the picture of our camp this is the way we lie the houses that can see that is the fort that we hafter qard you can see the canens the middle is our street the two hoses that is on the ends is the cook house you must keep it till I come home and then I can tell you all About it you son Joseph has ben her to day he is well and he seys that he had sent 20 dolars home And I member I was very glad to see him he looks very helthey and the rest of the boys he is About three miles from her but he dont now how long he will Stay their the colnel is A looking for A camp grond you must write to me and tell me if you hav got his 20 dolars then I can tell him for I cant tell you whare he will Stop we hav got our pay to day and we did not git the notes that I thought that we wold So I ges that I will wate A Spell before I sent mine home it is fun to See the boys by things and to see the pedlers the pedlers will hafter be smarter than I be to git mine money I think that I can keep money as well as the pedlers I giv ten sents for this paper to Send it home so you see how we live Joseph has not got his horse yet the cernel Shaull laft at him for be A Cavler and gonen A foot Joseph says that he was glad to get out of that please that he was in for it was so sickley I toll Joseph that I wold write to you and let you now how he got along and whare he was I hav Jes got that paper that come from Springfield what to you think of the paper that I sent to you I cant write much to say for their is such a call for money the boys are all runen with money in their hands some apaying their dets some of them a clecton in their dets and some A bian in gootes Joseph did not stay her long for he run A way and he had go back to See whare he was A gain So I bot him a pie and some cookeys and some cheas for his times then he went back I thought that I wood Giv him something goot so he wood come agin goote by

I now must close my leter for I hav no more knews Joseph sends his lov to you all and says that he will rite as soon as he gits setlel you must write all the knews and tell me whare the girles is and the boys they was A felow come her jus now and sed that they was A gonter to gard the sity the rigment that Joseph is in that will sute Joseph That is A bout five miles from her then we can see each other very often the day is now gon and I must close my leter please write as often as you can and I will to the same giv my lov to all the girls and to the boys and keep the bigest part for you and father

From your Son Lester K Winslow to John K Winslow

giv my lov to all the girles that is union girles tell them that I am yet single tell John to take good care of Lusinbay if I dont write an toote him musent tolk lov to her for I can do that

Letter from Amasa Cook Myrick of Gilbertsville to his Father June 10, 1862

Fort Worth

Dear Father

I received your kind letter on the 8 inst and now sit down to reply to it this was the first letter I have received from you in over four weeks in the same time I wrote you two if you received them and have answered them they must have been overlooked or mislaid, or miscarried or something as some of the boys letters come through as they should and some do not I am very well at present and so are the rest of the boys the climate agrees with us first rate there is not much sickness in camp now the weather is very warm the boys wear nothing but a shirt & pants & shoes the less clothing we have on the better we feel we do not drill and to speak of we get up at roll call at 5:00 and drill until 6 ½ with our rifles we are armed with the enfield rifles now and from 9 until 10 ½ on the siege guns in the fort and twice a week on batallion drill inspection and review General Whipple in command the rest of the day we have to ourselves to play ball or anything else. Our feed at present is none of the best but we get along very well

On last payday our Colonel gave the men three days to drink whiskey and get drunk or anything and of the most disgraceful sights my eye never witnessed but very few of our company got drunk the men were fighting and quarreling most all the time Our colonel came home from Alexandria one night pretty drunk and ordered the sergeant of the guard to put three trees under arrest thinking they were men this is our dutch Colonel I understand that the regiment is to be filled to the required number and we are to be light artillery yet we are to have the horses in a few days and the batteries when the horses are broke so much for the petition. We had strawberries ten days ago and plenty of them this is a great place for them peaches blackberries will soon follow When you write I wish yould tell me what is going on in the village I sent you ten dollars by express let me know whether you get it or not I sent you 15 dollars that I have never heard from 10 at one time 5 at another in a letter

Yours & C

Write soon

Please direct to A. C. Myrick 2nd Regt. N. Y. V. Arty Fort Worth Alexandria Va Company E care Capt Klinck be sure and put on these directions & there is no danger

Excerpt from a Letter from
Thomas F. Weldon of Richfield Springs to James Weldon
July 17, 1862

Camp Opposite Fredericksburg

Dear Brother

Does father work for Derthick this Summer and how does his house and lot look I suppose the farmers are paying now how does the Old man stand it I am going to Send home $100.00 Dollars as Soon as our next pay day Which will be in a week when so Does Dick send home any money Due you get the pictures I sent you if so do you think look any like the Subscriber we had a Shower last night and this morning it is cool and pleasant

Co. A have been doing Brigade guard duty at the Hed Qrts of Genl. Doubleday we had to be very particular to have our Boots straps blacked and our guns as bright as a Dollar the Major a Brother of the Genl inspects us and if there is a spot on the gun it has to be cleaned and the owner perhaps goes to the Guard House do you see Horace Sliter often if he give him my Respects also Mr & Mrs Slytus and family

now Jimmie write as soon as you get this and write me a good long letter write me all the news of the day and how things are at Home no more at Present I remain your
Affectinate Brother
Thos. F. Welden

PS Direct Your leters 76 Regt Co. K, Washington D.C.

Excerpt from the Diary of
Andrew Adrian Mather, Sheriff of Otsego County

Aug. 14, 1862
Went down to Garratsville at 8 o'clock to see soldiers off. Emmet and Elias for Mohawk, enlisted to fight for their country.

Aug. 19, 1862
Left town for Ilion and Mohawk. Took dinner at Ilion and drove down to Mohawk and saw the soldiers, staid there one hour, bid goodbye to Emmet and Elias. Felt as though it was the last time I should see them on earth, prayed to God that he would preserve them all from harm.

Aug. 21, 1862 (Middlefield)
Arrested a deserter by the name of Drew.

Aug. 23, 1862 (Mohawk)
I went to Albany and left Drew about 9 p. m. at the Barracks with Capt. Rice.

Aug. 25, 1862 (Cooperstown)
Arrested Stephen Sweet, a deserter, at Robinsons.

Aug. 30, 1862 (Schuylers Lake)
Arrested Timothy Herkimer for disloyalty, brought him down to jail. Writ of Habeas Corpus is applied for, shall not obey it if issued.

Sept. 1, 1862
Judge Nelson issued writ of Habeas Corpus today but I disregarded it. Am expecting a telegram from Turner. I shall take the bull by the horns. Arrested a deserter in Springfield 10 p. m. Zera has returned and

brought a dispatch from Turner to resist any effort to liberate Timothy Herkimer and report to him any person that helps in the matter.

Sept. 2, 1862
Refused to answer and make return to writ of Habeas Corpus.

Letter from
Captain John W. Young of Springfield to his Father
September 4, 1862

Dear Father:-

I have only time to write a few lines. I have attempted to write several times, but did not get a half a dozen lines written before we were ordered to move. We have been on the move since the 9th of August. I have not been able to get clean under clothes for three weeks until today. We have been in all the fights of importance in this section, except that of Cedar Mountain.

Five of our Captains are wounded, and two Lieutenants, one of whom has since died, viz: Lieut. Williams Capt. Swan is among the wounded. About half of our men are either killed, wounded, or missing. Our men behaved beautifully, and fought desperately. John Vorhees fell mortally wounded by my side. I think Lester Winslow is also killed. I have not heard of him since going into the first action.

Wash. Devoe, Charles W. Devoe, William G. Van Horne, were all severely wounded with a number more of my company from Otsego County. I have not time to give their names. I am the only Captain left in the Regiment, now, who is reported able for duty. Our Major was also seriously wounded, and a number of the boys were taken prisoners. They have been paroled, and some 1,500 passed through here yesterday for Washington, among whom were two or three of our regiment. They say they had hard fare – but I must close or I shall not be able to get this in the mail.

Excerpt from *The Cherry Valley Gazette*, September 10, 1862

Losses in the Seventy-Sixth N.Y.V.

We publish below a letter from Captain Swan, which was kindly furnished us to relieve the anxiety of those who have friends in the 76th.

Washington, Sept. 3

Dear Wife:-

Once more I am placed so I can communicate with you. I wrote a line from Manassas and sent by an officer who was going forward when I could not. He could walk and went on foot. I had to be carried, and was four days reaching here. I hope you got that letter as it must have relieved your anxiety. i am very comfortable this morning. My wound to be sure, is painful, but I think will soon heal. The ball entered the back part of my thigh near the hip and struck the bone so hard that it battered the ball up as if it had struck a rock. It must come very near indeed to shattering the bone. I has turned around at the moment to speak to the Colonel and Major, who were right behind me at the time. This saved my life; an instant sooner I was faced the other way, and if the ball had come then it would have struck in the groin or just below and severed the great artery, and all would soon been over.

I must tell all I know about the others of our company. It was a terrible fight for a short one. In less than one hour over half of two brigades were killed and wounded on our side. We were in about three-fourths of an hour and lost over one third of the Regiment in killed and wounded. Four Captains, the other three all worse than myself - one or two will die. Nine of Co. H were wounded that I know of, viz: Sergt. Jas. George, leg, slightly; Geo. Snow, leg, slightly; B.A. Campbell, right hand, badly; J.J. Reese, right fore finger C.R. Dingman, right thumb, amputated; Jay C. Stanton, legs; Byron Green, badly wounded but refused to be taken from the field. I fear he died. Wm. Miller, in foot, badly. This brave fellow lay on the ground in front of the company and continued to fire till all was over. Corporal Perry Oaks was killed instantly, at almost the first fire, by a ball through the head. There may be others, but I think not as I saw the Lieuts. the next day, and they knew of no more. None are dangerous except Green. Irving Baker, Albert Gross, Alf. Folen, and all the other village boys I know are safe and have seen them.

Excerpt from *Experiences and Activities of a Lifetime* by Henry Hilton Wood of Middlefield

Our regiment was put in an old brigade of the 6th Army Corps and the next day we started on our first march (a rush march) to meet General Lee's army that was crossing the Potomac at Harper's Ferry. It was a hard tramp for us. The sun was so hot and we were not used to marching. We met the enemy first at a pass in South Mountain, called Crampton's Pass. There I first heard the roar of cannon and screams of shot and shell. There, too, I saw the first dead soldier. The sight made me very sick. After awhile I became so accustomed to it that I could lay down and sleep with them all around me.

Letter from Amasa Cook Myrick of Gilbertsville to his Father September 10, 1862

Fort Bennett Va.

Dear Father

Received your letter day before yesterday and was very glad to hear that you were all well. My health is very good at present and I hope these few and hurried written lines may find you and the rest of the folks all well

We are at present garrisoning Fort Bennett just across the river at Georgetown District of Columbia we have got a very pleasant camp and not much to do at present

We have been living on hard crackers or as we call them hardees and salt horse for the last two weeks and sleeping on the ground sometimes with a blanket and sometimes without

It does not make much difference whether we can have a blanket or not for we have been sleeping on the ground all the while where ever we could get a chance to lie down we have now got tents and are to stay here some time. I have seen Genrl. McCleelan Genrl Fitz John Porter and Secretary Stannton within the past week Genrl Fitz John Porter was here at our fort on Sunday last and he liked our appearance first rate he made a few remarks and went his way I would not be surprised if we should have to leave here in a few days. Some of the boys are satisfied with seeing one battle but I am not it makes me more anxious to see another but in a different shape and end a little different than the first one. This retreating I do not like when they go in such a hurry I like to hear the shells and shot whistle by but not to come to close.

They generally plough a pretty deep furrough and pretty wide. Our company is in the fort alone and we have good times. When the Regiment came off the Battle field Capt Klinck had one of the colors and it is reported that he threw it away how true it is I do not know but it is just like him do not let this get abroad that I wrote this to you

Yours & C
A. Cook M

Excerpt from a Letter from
John S. Kidder of Laurens to his wife, Harriet Kidder
(in *Subdued by the Sword* by James M. Greiner)
15 September 1862

About 9,000 of our men, comprised of Bartlett's, (Brig. Gen. John) Newton and part of (Brig. Gen. William) Smith's Brigades went up to fight the enemy and take the (Crampton's) pass. Gen. Slocum said he would do it in half an hour after he got within reach of them. I think he carried it in less than that time after he commenced firing. They made a splendid charge up a hill as Cooley's and utterly routed them. It was an exciting scene to witness. The enemy were posted at the foot of the hill in the woods which is composed of trees, (there was) no under brush to obstruct the passage of our men. I was fearful it would be night before the attack could be made but the fight was finished before dark. We came over the field early this morning. I counted 156 dead Rebels and 39 of our men besides any quantity of wounded while coming up the hill. I think I counted about all the dead of our men, as most of them were killed before they reached the woods. The Rebels lay strewn all along up the hill; they had a very strong position and ought to have held the pass with 500 men with their batteries, but they ran like sheep.

Letter from
Andrew Chisholm of Burlington to his sister, Nettie Cornell
October 4, 1862

Camp near Sharpsburg

Sister Nettie

As the mail goes out today I will write a few lines. I received fathers letter last Saturday and I want to hear from home worse than ever now as I long to know how Robert is. My health has been tolerable good most of the time but I was a little of the hinges yesterday but I feel a little better this morning. It is nothing serious I guess only my Stomach is a little out of order. I am not bad enough to drill and do other duty all the time. We have been in the same place for about ten days now and the prospect is we will stay some time as we are to have shelter tents in a few days. They have put us right through the drilling since we have been here.

We were reviewed by the President in person yesterday afternoon. There was three divisions all in one field and this is quite a number as four regiments make a brigade and three brigades make a division. We were drawn in a line eight files deep and Uncle Abe rode along the lines with hat in hand and smiling in a very fatherly manner. He was accompanied by the field officers belonging to the divisions. There was a salute of twenty-two guns fired in honor of him. He rode on a neat little black horse and he was dressed in a plain black suit. I do not think he is near as homely as I have heard him represented to be. Although he is lean and gaunt he looks as if his business wore upon him. There was a man of Co. G from Cherry Valley died last Thursday morning. His name was Parsons. He was buried at dusk. It was about as solem an affair as I ever witnessed. The procession was led by two files of soldiers four abrest and the band followed next and they played one of the solemnest tunes on muffled drums that I ever heard. Thomas Adams and some boys that were left at Washington came in yesterday. They look very white compared with the rest of us. Rufuses Nephew a fellow by the name of Bemis was among them. You may tell Rufus he is well if you see him. The nights are getting to be very cool but the days are warm enough. There has only been about three days that it has rained in all the time we have been out. We are close by a mill and we bought a little flour and made some pancakes which tasted first rate after eating hardtack so long and we got a few ears of corn from a cornfield close by and we made a grater out of a piece of tin and grated meal and we made porridge and if I ever ate good porridge and molasses that was it. I wear two shirts at a time so I wash one at a time and by so doing get along very well. But I have only one pair of socks with me so I have to go slip shod until they dry. This is the greatest place for bugs and spiders that I ever saw. I cannot lay down but they will be crawling all over me and you may imagine what an agreeable feeling they have. I have not found any lice on me yet but expect I will get them for the old soldiers around here are covered with them. I often see them sitting with their shirts off picking them off. Willie Elliott is well and appears to enjoy himself very well. When any of you write just mention how Uncle Johns folks are if you have seen any of them. Elias Mather is rather unwell he is threatened with a fever and our Captain has not been able to get out for a day or two. Tell the rest of the girls to write me. I think they need not be so particular about me writing first and if you do not always get an answer right along write again but I will always try to answer the letters I get. I have only had two yet and I think that is rather few for the time I have been gone and the number I have written. Give my kindest respects to father and mother and all the rest of the folks. Write soon as I want to hear from Robert. You had better dry lots of pumpkins and save some apples for if I should happen to be home between now and next spring there would be no supplying me.

A. Chisholm

Direct
Washington D. C., Co. K. 121 regt. N. Y. S. V. Bartletts Brigade

Letter from Amasa Cook Myrick of Gilbertsville to his Father October 5, 1862

Fort Bennett

Dear Father

You will be anxious I know to hear from me as I have been from you I received your letter yesterday and read the contents in a hury and was sorry to hear that Mrs Coss was dead. I am also glad to hear that Ed. Gilbert is Captain and also that Willard is first Lieut. And I suppose that he has got a full company and ready for a drill &C The weather here is very warm in the day time but is pretty cold in the night time and we have very heavy dews and fogs.

The people around here say that the country around here is not very healthy the boys are beginning to have the fever and ague three of the boys in our company have had a slight touch ague which luckily for them has been broken up and they are all well now they had markely the shake in the for noon between the hours of nine and eleven A. M. and between eight and ten P. M.

You spoke about fixing the house now and I think it is a very good plan providing you can do so with-out running in debt a great deal but when you do it – do it well and put on a good shingle roof I suppose money is pretty scarce now with you and just now it is here and also in the treasury we have not been paid in over two months and now have three months pay due us but cannot tell when we shall get it but when it comes I will send you all I can have to spare to help rig up the house There has been an order posted up in the Paymaster department not to pay any more troops at present for their fund are getting short they have been paying for arms &C but will not last but a few days at most and I think we will be the first to be paid being so near to Washington only across the river in regard to giving money in bounties to these new regiments is a great shame and I ask you not to give one red cent to the people if the way to give they had better give to the old soldiers now in the field they are the ones that need and deserve it and do not make any clothes or send any to regiments for the soldiers for three fourths of the things never reach the soldiers the officers get hold of these things and keep them for themselves, and if you do send anything send it by express if we stay in these forts this winter the boys in this tent will send home for some things before a great while such as clothing &C

From your son
A. Cook Myrick

Excerpt from a Letter from Samuel D. French to his Sister October 5, 1862

There is something peculiar about a soldiers life. He is liable to be called into line at any time with a moment's notice and for that reason it is almost impossible to write a letter without being called away before it is finished. You notice, I have at different times yesterday I was called away for inspection of arms and last night it rained enough to prevent writing but not enough to lay the dust but made it a little cooler. I never saw a pleasanter day than today, and I was never more entertained than I am here. It will sound rather rough to you, but I do not mind it. I have not been inside of a house nor slept under a tent in a month, but have slept in the grass and have not had a sore throat nor a cold since I left Camp Schuyler. Some of the boys make calculations on being discharged soon on account of the reported offers of peace by the confederates which you have probably seen, but I cannot foresee peace yet.

Excerpt from a Letter from
Andrew Chisholm of Burlington to his sister, Nettie Cornell
October 21, 1862

Camp near Bakersville

Sister Nettie

Your letter of the eleventh came to hand yesterday and I was glad to hear from you for I had about come the conclusion that you were not agoin to write to me at all

On Saturday we received orders to move so we packed up our tents & blankets and marched about one mile & a half toward the river and camped on a very pleasant situation and got our tents all pitched and everything slicked up & on Sunday there was a devine Service which I attended & on Monday forenoon we got orders to march back to our old camp ground again. So back we went & now we are under orders to be ready to march at any moment but for all that we may not have to move.

We received our knapsacks on Monday and my things came all right except my dress coat that was lost but I have got another one. It was one which belonged to a boy who has deserted & the clothes were divided among those who had lost any of their clothes. Today we received our overcoats so I guess we will be able to keep warm now. The weather has been very cool lately & it was quite a frost this morning. If we could happen to have to march any distance with the load we have got now it will give us a hard one but then we have got to stand everything & a person doesn't know how much he can endure until he is obliged to try it. I have never said much about our Co. officers but I will say to you that our Capt. is one of the greatest blockhead that I ever saw. In fact he does not know anything worth mentioning. Lieut. Mather is as good an officer as ever need to be. He learns the drill very quick & has got a good faculty of explaining it to the men & he is very friendly and good natured among the boys. Our second Lieut. is rather a rough cursing sort of a fellow yet there is a good deal of snap in him I am in hopes he will not be in Command a great while. He is very afraid to have the Colonel come I think he is afraid of being thrown out of his position. Billie Elliott had been quite sick but he is considerable better now but he is not able to do duty yet he was threatened with a fever. Elias is getting better. Albert Chase is tough and hearty. George Pierson is quite sick, I believe the rest of the boys that you know are well. As for myself I have no reason to complain. Charlie Mather & Delos Eddy got here today they have had quite a time in getting here they were arested as being deserters & locked up once or twice. H. Whitford also got here today. He has had quite an easy time at the hospital & had plenty to eat & of good quality he is the fleshiest that I ever saw him. Rant Bennett wants you to tell Alvas folks to write to him he has written to them but has not received any answer from them. You spoke about sending things. If our folks has a chance to send anything I wish they would send my winter vest & a silk pocket handkerchief for I have lost nearly all of mine & the next most exceptable thing is dried fruits of any kind but I guess they had better wait until we get into winter quarters if that time should ever come. You spoke of me coming home on a furlough but I do not want to come until the Rebellion is put down if my health is good but I would like to help to eat those dried plums. I will give you a short list of prices down here. Cheese 25 cents per pound, Soda Crackers 25 cents per pound, Potatoes 4 cents per pound, Bread 25 cents per loaf, Whiskey 12 shillings per quart bottle & other things in proportion. But I guess I had better stop as it is nearly dark & as I have written this very poorly it will be enough for you to read at once. Give my respects to Peleg and all other enquiring friends write soon & give me as many news as you did last time

Yours
A Chisholm

Excerpt from a Letter from
Andrew Chisholm of Burlington to his sister, Nettie Cornell
November 16th, 1862

Camp near New Baltimore
Virginia

Sister Nettie

I received your letter of the second last Wednesday & was glad to hear that you were all well. I also received one from Jane. She is well as usual. I wrote a letter to father last Monday & since then we have not marched any. They seem to be determined to let all this fine weather pass without doing anything & then when it comes wet muddy weather we will probably have to tramp again, but then I suppose it is none of our business, all we have to do is to obey orders. I have learned to never ask any questions but just wait until we receive an order and then prepare to execute it as speedily as possible. There is one thing about soldiering it learns a man to be independent the fastest of any business that I ever was in. Everyone has got to lookout for himself for if he does not he will be apt to far slim.

Our whole corps which consists of about forty thousand men are now camped around within bugle sounding distance so you may judge there is considerable stir going on the whole of the time and when the camp fires are all lighted up at night they present rather a beautiful appearance. We are about two miles from the Alexandria & Manassas junction railroad so it is quite handy to receive our supplies from.

I used to dread the thoughts of marching with my knapsack & tent cloth but I find I can stand it to carry them all this cool weather full as well as when we had only our blankets and gun equipage when it was so warm. I think the health of the regiment is a good deal better since the cool weather. I have not heard from Billie Elliott since he was sent to Harpers Ferry therefore I know nothing about how he is getting along. Emmet had a letter from Elias yesterday. He is at Hagerstown. He is getting quite well again. He is able to be around town on business part of the time. I hear that some of the boys write home some pretty hard stories of how they fare and complain that they do not get half enough to eat, but I think they must either give a false report or then it requires a great deal more to sustain them than it does me. Of course it is not of the nicest kind but there has never been a time but what my old haversack has contained a quantity of government shingles, and we generally have port or fresh meat in abundance. We had rations of dried apples which we stewed up and sweetened well and they proved to be a grand treat. Beans are about the best of anything that we get. I have not tasted soft bread since I got into Virginia. If Peleg expects to be in this business before long I guess I will give him a little advice. First he had better learn to live without milk for he will not get any here and it will be easier to break off gradualy that to dry off at once. Second he had better have his teeth well filled if they need it and have new ones put in the vacant places if there is any such for Uncle Sam's hard tack takes a good deal of chewing, but there is one advantage which they have, that is it require very few of them to sustain a man. Three with a little meat and a cup of coffee will make a good meal. Also a pair of good boots and mittens are fine things. Tell him that I hope he will not be offended at me for what I have written as I do not mean to disparage. I guess Ellen must be mad about something for I have not heard a word from her since I wrote her. It is a lucky thing for your chickens that I can not get among them for soldier boys have got a great faculty for severing their heads from their bodies, but I must close and get my dinner ready.

I remain your affect. Brother
A. Chisholm

Letter from Cyrus J. Hardaway of Pittsfield to his Mother November 21, 1862

Near Fredericksburg Va

Dear Mother

It is just one year today since I left home and I think I am seeing hard times than I ever saw before. We started from Warrenton last Monday in the rain and it has rained every day and night since. My clothes and blankets have been wet through all the time. It had not rained any now for about two hours and I have got partly dried. I am all out of Tobacco and money and no prospect of getting any more for a good while don't know what I shall do. Can you send me some don't think you can for I can't get any mail. Think I am pretty hard up don't you think so They say that we cant have any winter quarters yet a while. I think we could do just as well in good winter quarters as we can tramping around in the mud up to our knees. They say that McClellan was removed because he proposed going into winter quarters it may be all right but I cant see it, in that light. We have tramped back over the same road that we went up on last August. It would not be much of a wonder if we had to go back up there again and have another battle at bull run. As near I can find out the rebs occupied Warrenton the same day that we left. There was firing there shortly after we left and I presume they overtook our rear guard. Old Abraham has got his hands full and the quicker he makes a compromise the better it will be for him. You never can lick the buggers out. That's a sure thing. If you can read this letter you can do a great deal better than I can, so I think I might as well stop.

Your aff Son
CJH

Excerpt from a Letter from John S. Kidder of Laurens to his wife, Harriet Kidder (in *Subdued by the Sword* by James M. Greiner) November 27, 1862

I expect to have a hand in the fight at Fredericksburg. If you should hear that I am killed or wounded you must not believe it until you hear it from some reliable source. And if it should be my lot to fall, mourn not for me but take care of my girl and bring her up as she should be brought up. Educate her well by all means and she will be a comfort to you.

Yours as ever, J. S. Kidder

Excerpt from *Experiences and Activities of a Lifetime* by Henry Hilton Wood of Middlefield

We moved down some distance into Virginia and camped awhile. Here I was selected as drummer-boy, together with seven other boys about my size and age. A teacher was furnished us. After practicing a few days, we received orders to move in the morning. A cold December rain was pouring down, but we marched, wet through. About four o'clock in the afternoon it began to snow. We left the high and wooded land and went down on wet, marshy lowland close to the arm of Chesapeake Bay, we were ordered to stay there. There was no wood to make a fire to warm ourselves by or to make coffee, nothing to eat but hardtack. Our clothes were freezing to us. That was the worst night we saw while in the service. Men grew sick and died because of that awful night at Belle Plain. We had been sent there to guard the ships that were to land supplies for the army. We moved on to Fredericksburg where

Lee's army was in a strong position on the hills and the Rappahannock River flowed between us and the foe.

A great battle was fought here, and the Union Army lost heavily. After the battle, we went back about three miles and fixed our camp for the winter; and there I learned to play the drum.

Letter from Amasa Cook Myrick of Gilbertsville to his Father December 12, 1862

Fort Worth

Dear Father

I received your letter of the 9th on the 11th stating that you were in good health and am glad to hear it. I have enjoyed exceedingly good health but at present have got a very bad cold and it has settled on my lungs and every time I cough it seems as if there was some needles sticking into me I might go to the hospital but I had rather lay in my tent and rot first for our doctor is drunk a greater part of the time and neglects his patients There is a disease coming among us called the measles and two of the Birdsall boys have got them. We have to stand guard every other day now for some 15 or so of the boys are sick and the rest of us that are left have to drill on the guns or are on fatigue. You will have a chance to send those boots with other. Sykes Donaldson Chas. A Hurlbutt Gilbert Birdsall, Byron Duce Fred Howard and others have sent home for boots and things and we will have them sent together. You can see Henry Donaldson about it he is going to send home to Sykes. Our pickets were drive in night before last and the rebels are about 3 or 4 miles from us and we expect an attack almost daily and I not care how soon they come We are drilling in the for on the big guns and riffed and parrot guns, and we have got so that we can work them pretty well, well enough to kill all the rebels that dare come within shooting distance You are probably [aware] that this fort is originally called fort taylor and Beauregard swears that he will have it but he can never get while we are here. The fort is in such condition now that it can not be taken without a considerable loss of life to the rebels there are two other forts that can have a sweep at them at the same time this went by the name of star fort for it is in the shape of a star. Perhaps you have seen the general order of McClelland in regard to enlisted men of these older than 45 and under 21 and especially under 18 that their captains are to pay for their clothes and their wages up to the time of their discharge and their bounty money and if this is the case some of the captains in Morgan's artillery will be some what out of pocket and no loose change to spare. The times are such now that we can not go out side of camp guard with a pass for more than 8 or 10 hours at the most and 4 chances to one that we can get a pass at all. We have uncommon fine weather here it being as warm now as it is in Gilbertsville in the summer time.

Give my respects to all and I remain yours truly

   A C Myrick

Excerpt from a Letter from Elijah Keith of Milford to his wife, Caroline
December 24, 1862

                                    Fort Henry, Wednesday eve

Dear Wife:

I thought seeing I had written to you twice in a week, I would write to Celia tonight, but here it is to you again well my only excuse is I can't help it, and you must put up with it just as I have to with unpleasant things. You say you would like to come and make me a visit, I should like to have you call a few days at our pleasant little village and see how soldiers fare, and I can see no good reason for your staying at home you can come without a pass and I can not go home without one if I could I should go mighty quick. I don't know as I am disappointed any, I expected to be lonesome and anxious to be at home with my family but I thought I could endure it, and I think so yet, but I think if you were situated as I am, and I as you are, I should do otherwise as you propose to do; tho I appreciate your kind offer to come and take care of me if sick, that might be well, but it may be when the sickness comes, it will be to late, as it was with Freeman Rose, all to be seen, a corpse.

Late event of the war are not very encouraging and what the end will be and when it will be is more than I can tell one thing I know, it is the accursed sin of slavery that has brought this horrible war upon us and those that have been quiet, and perhaps had some sympathy for the institution have rendered aid, and encouragement to the enemies of our country; in fact they have strengthened the hands of the rebels and the late victories of the mock democracy in the northern states is just what pleases the rebels and I have my fears that it will have a tendency to protract the war; if the rebels know that half of us are really with them in sympathy they will hold out with more courage and determination and ten to one if it does not end in a disgraceful compromise. But I am not to blame about is I enlisted in good faith and if we fail to accomplish any good it will be on account of designing men working against the government in secret connexion with the rebels.

Excerpt from *The Freeman's Journal*, January 9, 1863

Another box of mittens was forwarded by the Ladies of this place to the Soldiers of the 152d Regiment on Tuesday last. The Soldiers have a good friend in Miss L. Pickens of this village, who has taken principal charge of this matter.

Col. Upton says that the present pressing wants of the soldiers of the 121st Regt. is blankets, coverlids, sheets and pillow cases and tick. To supply this want as speedily as possible, let those who have friends in the 121st Regt., bring such of these articles as they can spare to Cockett & Marvin, labeled with the name of the person intended for. Some may feel willing to contribute of these necessary articles, leaving Col. Upton to distribute them to those needing them. A small sum, perhaps twenty-five cents more or less, should be left with each package for defraying expenses of boxing and transportation; if it should prove more than necessary the balance will be paid over to the soldiers. Those things are needed immediately by the soldiers of the 121st Regt. If the Regt. remains where it is, or goes into winter quarters, these comforts will be enjoyed by them until the warm weather renders them unnecessary. In case of the advance of the army they might have to be thrown away, or lost; but Col. Upton says that the friends of soldiers ought to be willing to take the risk. I wish an abundance of these things to be sent in to Cockett & Marvin's during the coming week. They will see to boxing and forwarding them without delay.

J. B. Wood

Excerpt from a Letter from John W. Ballard of Cherry Valley to his Brother and Sister Camp near Fredericksburg February 2, 1863

Dear Brother and Sister,

We have got very bad weather down here now. We have had a foot of snow. But it is all gone now. Alf Nichols has Run a Way and a great many more out of Our Regiment. But I guess there was no more that you knew. He was gone ten days Before I knew that he was gone. Moses and Menzo are well and Rob Fox and Sam French are well also.

Our Men is a runing a Way and a Dying off so fast that We have not got More than four hundred Men left fit for duty. I think that is a decreasing prity fast don't you. We have not had Only five Men killed and eleven wounded in Battle and the rest has ben left sick and dyed and run a way.

I should like too see you and the children. Tell liby that her uncle John is a going to have that Man took off his arm when he come home. She will not bee a fraid off him any more. I should like too have you Rite too Me When you get this if you think I am deserving of it and I will Rite too you a gain. Give my best Respects too all. So No More at present.

From you Brother
John W. Ballard

Excerpt from the Diary of
Andrew Adrian Mather, Sheriff of Otsego County

Feb 25, 1863

After dinner drove down to Westville to serve a summons and called on Simonds folks. Found them Secesh. Drove up to John Hinds and had a good visit.

Letter from
William H. Chapin of New Lisbon to his sister, Charlotte
Camp near White Oak Church
February 27, 1863

Dear Sister Charlotte

It was with pleasure that I received a letter from you dated January 27. It came to hand last Monday. I was vaccinated yesterday to prevent small pox. Today I have been on a detail of 14 men cutting wood for the officers. Have just got back so I thought I would improve the time while the regiment is out on drill in writing to you. My health is tolerable good now but chopping is a little to hard for me yet. It is the first duty I have done in sometime. We now draw three days rations at a time consisting of one or more loaves of soft bread and hard crackers to make out. Pork and fresh and salt beef one days each. Coffee and once in a long time poor tea. Sugar Raisins. Beans, potatoes and some stuff for making soup. So you can see we are living much better than we did a few months ago altho it is a great way from what I am used to get at home as butter and cheese and other articles are very often through of in getting our meals. I will first give you a short list of a few articles here. Butter nothing short of 50 cts lb. Cheese good 40cts second rate 30 cts lb. Apples 5 for 25 cts oranges 3 or 4 for 25 cts lemons about the same daily paper two days old 10 cts boots 8 to $15 a pair pies round 40 cts fried cakes 2 1/2 cts each small biscuit 40 cts a dozen. The weather is very changeable of late. It either snows or rains nearly every other day with once in a while a pleasant day. It is terrible muddy now. We have a company regimental and brigade inspection tomorrow. The peddlers from the old regiments are terrible thick in camp since being off. They and the old suttlers will get the biggest part of the money paid to the regiment if we are not paid soon. The health of the regiment is very good now and if the smallpox does not get to doing its work I shall be glad. As a specimen of what roads are I will tell you what is a load for a good four horse or a six mule team. The wood is cut and split (oak) five or six feet long and they put in one length about as much as it would take to fill up in Father's old lumber wagon box until it is long enough. Time passes very fast but I do not see that the cause in which we are engaged in goes as fast as it ought to. My best respects to all from your affectionate brother.

Wm. H. Chapin

Letter from
Thomas F. Weldon of Richfield Springs to James Weldon
March 9, 1863

Camp Near Pratts Point Va.

Dear Brother

Your letters of the 2nd and 3rd arrive to hand to night I hasten to reply not hearing from you I wrote a few days sins thinking perhaps you did not receive the letter I wrote sending for the Box and I thought had better not Send it as it would take Some time to get the Boots made but as it is all ready it will be in time I was glad to hear that the package of money reached Home in Safety as My no hearing from you did not know but it ought not have reached you

I Should Judge from your letter Wages must be high and that Bill is among the best of them to be able to Command $18 per month the weather to day has been warm and the air so soft and Balmey as if were the Middle of may

I believe I have never Given you a description of our house it is about 10 feet Square and built of logs Split with an ax so to resemble boards as much as posablewell the logs are up about 6 feet high then Covered with Shelter tents and rubber Blankets so that it is secure against any storm then at one Side we have a good large fire place made of poles cut about four feet long and lane up high enough to make a chimney then our Bunk is made of poles and Covered with fine Ceder Boughs for feathers and I have 3 Army Blankets and my tent Chum 2 making 5 so I would not ask to Sleep better than we do

Our Rations are much better then they were we are now furnished with good Soft-bread fresh from the ovens and we get Potatoes & onions three times per Week plenty of Coffee and Sugar lots of pork and beef we have as much as 30 lbs of pork in the Shanty and we have to throw it away then we get beans rice Hominey & upon the whole the rations are very good while in Camp but tough on the march I never enjoyed beter Health in my life then I do at the present time I think I never was so fleshey

the fifes and drums have Just struck up Yankee Doodle for revelee and I must go and Call the roll and as it is about nine 0'clock I must bid you good night until Some Other time

Thos F. Welden

Excerpt from "War Reminiscences" by Delevan Bates (published in *The Otsego Republican*, October 25, 1895)

In April [1863] the regiment was sent by steamer to Suffolk Va., and here they received the first idea of what war really was. Gen. Longstreet was besieging the city. The weather was rainy, the soil sandy, and underlying the surface was a brackish water not fit to drink. Malarial fever came and the hospital was soon filled. Under arms night and day, an occasional skirmish but no heavy battles made the time pass very interesting, but not particularly enlarging the death list, as but few were killed.

Letter from Thomas Smith to L. W. Rathbun
Camp near White Oak Church
April 12, 1863

I take my pen in hand to inform you of my health wich is good at present hoping these few lines will find you and your family the same perhaps you would like to know what we are up to we are still in camp on the old ground the weather is quite warm to day wich the boys call Joe Hookers day but it rains from one to two days in a week wich the boys call the soldiers day for one rainy day converts hard solid ground into vast pools of mud and water into wich an empty wagon will sink to the hub last week we went out on review and we were reviewed by the President & Gen Hooker who were accompanied by the Presidents Wife and son it was a fine day and we had a nice time of it, Levant how does that big boy of yours get along does he walk alone yet. I showld like to see some of the conscripts down here as we hear a good deal about them but I have not seen any of them yet when they come they will know the reason why the arms does not move Phil Woodcock and the Wood boys are well I have two bone rings for my Wife and my little girl wich I will put in this letter for them to show what the soldier is up to during his leisure hours you wanted to know what regs form this Brigade they are the 27th & 16 N. Y. Vo. 5th Maine & 96th P. V. Coal heavers. I want you to tell my Wife that I want her to send me some Black linnen thread in the next letter she sends to me I close by sending my best respects to you your family and all enquiring friends
    Yours Truly,
    Thomas Smith

Letter from William H. Chapin of New Lisbon to his Sister
Camp near White Oak Church
April 16, 1863

Dear Sister

    I received your and George letter yesterday. It was the first since the one from Levonia of March 15th. I am not very well lately. Yesterday the Colonel ordered that every man should shave his face except the upper lip and that be allowed to grow. Was out on picket three days. Came in Saturday 2 PM. Am glad you got the prise for not whispering but guess you whispered once in awhile on the sly. It seems that you have not made much sugar at last account. Should think that you would have to be about it if you make much this season. It is getting so late. Got a letter last night from Uncle Wm. Was glad to hear from him again. I suppose that their young soldier is a great pet with them and makes them start when he speaks. I suppose you have grown to be quite a large girl by this time. It is less than eight months since I last saw you. Hope I can be at home less than eight more as I like the old spot more than soldiering. March 7th today we made a good deal of fuss in getting ready to be reviewed by General Hooker and the president but after we were ready the order came that there would not be any review today so we get the trouble for our paines. Only Talbert started for home this morning on furlough of ten days. I sent two pair of mittens by him to be left at Hoags harness shop Garrattesville. They were worth nothing to me this season. It is so late so I sent them home. I would not carry them through the season for them. Yesterday there was a grand cavalry charge. They passed by us a string of them more than a mile long to it. The talk is we shall be paid off again this week.

from your brother
Wm Chapin

Excerpt from *Experiences and Activities of a Lifetime* by Henry Hilton Wood of Middlefield

The first day of May [1863] we made another attack on Fredericksburg, under our new Commander, Joe Hooker. He took the army around Lee's left flank, all except the 6th Corps, which was to attack Fredericksburg when he had drawn most of Lee's troops after him. Our Regiment was in the 6th Corps. This plan was carried out. We took Fredericksburg and the fortified heights, and then passed on toward Richmond, but Hooker was defeated and Lee turned his whole force against us. In a battle near Salem Church our regiment was almost annihilated, especially my company. Out of seventy-seven men only seven answered roll call next morning; the others were killed, wounded or missing. Nine of these young men went from Middlefield Center, New York; only one answered roll call. My brother, John, was among the wounded.

All the next day they tried to capture the 6th Corps. Again and again we stopped them and then retreated to another place. That night we got across the Rappahannock River and joined the rest of the army. We went back to our old camp and remained there about six weeks. During that time Lee's Army was very active; they raided our wagon train in which my two brothers were drivers and they narrowly escaped being captured. They took 200 mules and about thirty drivers; none of these men were ever heard of again. The enemy cut our line of communication. Our brigade, consisting of five regiments and a battery of artillery was sent back about thirty miles along the railroad to guard it. While there a force of cavalry came in the night and charged our camp. The men were all asleep except myself. I heard the first shots as they ran through the picket line which was doing guard duty and heard the clatter of their horses feet while running. I grabbed my drum and began beating the long roll, which is a signal of warning that the enemy is at hand. By my presence of mind and quick warning I saved many lives, including the life of the General, commanding the force. The foe struck the camp near where I was still beating the drum, and fired at me. Our soldiers were making it so hot for them that they hurried to headquarteres to capture our General, but our men were so close after them that they could not stop to get him, so they fired a volley at his tent. He had heard my drum and had crawled out from under the back of the tent and ran behind an old corn crib. There were twenty ball holes through his tent about where he had been. He surely would have been killed had I not awakened him with the sound of my drum. He himself said I saved his life.

Excerpt from a Letter from Lansing B. Paine of New Lisbon to his Parents Near the Heights of Fredericksburg May 4, 1863

Dear Parents

Yesterday was a terrible day to the boys of the 121st. We arose about 1 o'clock, advanced our lines to the Richmond turnpike. About daylight cannonading commenced, the fifth Maine and our Reg were in a ravine. The enemy commenced shelling us and soon poured grape and canister. This first one wounded was Elias. He was hit by a bullet in the arm. It entered below the elbow and came out near the shoulder. It has not injured the bone, but will be a sore arm on account of the warm weather. About noon the right brigade stormed the heights and gained possession of them. Bartlett then took us through Fredericksburg up the hill. Our skirmishers were driving the rebels before them. Our division followed in line of battle. About half an hour before sundown we came to a piece of woods. The skirmishers were firing very rapidly.

Lansing Paine

Our division was ordered by Brooks to go through the woods. We advanced behind some obstructions, we marched beyond the skirmishers and halted a few rods from them and then the slaughter commenced. They poured volley after volley into us but the 121st did not retreat until the old Regiment did. For the reason of a flank fire. I will give you the names of the New Lisbon and Burlington boys that stood so manfully before so galling a fire. We did not have any panic in our ranks but retired until we came to a fence then rallied and the grape and canister strewed the ground with rebels from our batteries. We then with about sixty of our Reg and a few Jerseys and the 96th Penn., retook a house that the Rebels were around and held it. I do not think there was one from our way that did not die as soldiers should. The boys say that Mr Bow was the first one killed on Co K. He was shot in the head. How I escaped the volley of bullets is known only to God. I thought nothing of bullets and only to rally the men and have them rout the rebels. Once they did turn their back and if our whole brigade had remained steady we might have drove them. We ought to have charged bayonets when we first entered the woods. What makes it more horrible we could not hold our ground and was unable to know the fate of our comrades. I feel like avenging the deaths and so no man must talk to me of Southern Brethren, men who have murdered my schoolmates and companions. Co. K. went in with fifty seven they have only twenty one now the rest are killed wounded or missing. All the file closes of Co. E were wounded excepting Sergnt Woodcock and myself. I feel rather gloomy but shall try to do my duty manfully. I may get killed before this great battle is over but my life is in the hands of a higher power.

LB Paine

Excerpt from a Letter from
John S. Kidder of Laurens to his wife, Harriet Kidder
(in *Subdued by the Sword* by James M. Greiner)
May 4th, 1863

Battlefield West of Fredericksburg

Dear Wife,

It is with a sad heart I pen you a few lines having been through a most terrible battle and lost many of my men although I have come out unharmed. I had my pistol shot off from my belt which I lost and I had one bullet pass through my blanket and one through my pants just above my foot.

After we crossed over to Fredericksburg, we lay there to attract the attention of the Rebs until Saturday afternoon. About 6 o'clock we drove in their pickets, while Hooker was up north or west of them with five corps of the Army. What success he has had we do not know. On Saturday night we prepared to storm the heights above the city, started at 2 o'clock in the morning on Sunday. Our Regiment supported the left while some of the Vermont and New Jersey with the 43rd New York carried the heights and the U. S. Flag was planted in their forts by eleven o'clock A. M.

After we reached the top of the hill, our brigade formed the front line of battle to pursue the Rebs. We marched about 2 miles and found them posted in a wood. We gave battle. It was about 5 o'clock P. M. when we commenced the fight. We routed them at first and made a charge on them, and routed them until they came up to their 2nd line of battle. Then such a fire as we rec'd. has not been witnessed in this war, and is said by all the old soldiers and officers as being the very worst fire ever rec'd. from the rebels. The 23rd New Jersey joined us on our right but would not advance into the woods and after the fight commenced (they) immediately turned and ran like sheep, such miserable cowards ought to be shot. This caused the Rebels, who were in front of the Regt. to pour across and fire on our right wing. We were then ordered to retire to our 2nd line, and, as there were many tops of trees and limbs, we could not keep a good line and were somewhat scattered. A few cowards ran like sheep but most of the men retired without confusion. I am sorry to report that Zebulon Bowen ran about 1 1/2 miles and was stopped and arrested by the Provost Guard, The boys say he is a coward, and I have 2 men from Worcester and one from Hartwick that acted cowardly. Otherwise, my men behaved splendidly and fought like tigers.

After we came out of the woods, we retreated about 200 rods then made a rally around the colors with our Col. (who is one of the best and bravest hero). There were about 75 men of our Regt. and the Major of the 96th Pennsylvania with 15 of his men that rallied around our colors and succeeded in driving back the Rebels into the woods. The 2nd line of battle that was back of us did not support us properly and, if it had not been more for our Col. with his band of 75 men (for I think that there was not more than that number), it would have been a roust.

I shall never forget the noble fellows who stood by at that moment and fought until dark and I am proud to say that. Co. I had 14 men of that number and 2 officers. I will send you a list of their names who stood by me like brothers and fought so nobly.

I had 7 killed, 19 wounded, and 5 missing besides both of my Lieuts. wounded. I had only 55 men go into the fight besides 2 Lieuts. Is not this a terrible record? And our doctor went over to the ground which the Rebels held, and he says that they had many more killed and wounded than we had.

Charles F. Pattengill and Isaac Peck of Milford were not in the fight, for they volunteered in the morning while we were about to leave the left, to take a very exposed and dangerous position on a knoll to watch the movements of the enemy where they were exposed to grape and canister from one of their batteries and also their sharpshooters and they are entitled to as much credit as any for performing their duty nobly and bravely. Leroy Hall and Sedate Foote were with the Doctor to help take care of the wounded.

Letter from Amasa Cook Myrick of Gilbertsville to his Father May 8, 1863

Fort Bennett

Dear Father

I sit down to write to you a few lines for I have nothing else to do and have something to write about

Fred Howard is writing a letter to J. L. Gilbert & Co. which upon their receipt it will pay to you thirty dollars which amount I send to you hoping you will use it for yourself. When you write again please to let me know if you can use the amount sum total that I have sent for I take pleasure in sending this to you knowing by my wish that you will use it expressly for yourself

While I am writing the thunder rolls and the lightning flashes and the rain comes down almost in torrents and our canvas house leaks pretty bad

And for the past few days the thunder of Artillery & musketry is belching forth its music down on the Rappahannock and tells on the rebel ranks with fearful effect the slaughter must be great

Between seven and eight hundred prisoners arrived in Washington yesterday and one hundred of Mosbys guerillas and to day eight hundred more from the front The grand army of the Potomac for once has met with great success under our ablest and best commander "Old Fighting Joe Hooker" we are not in possession of the City of Fredericksburg and Gordonsville and part of our army are between the rebels and Richmond I expect to hear next that the rebel capitol is in our hands the railroad between Gordonsville and Richmond is cut off if this rain does not affect the army there will be some heavy fighting I have not heard from George in some time and do not know where he is at present

Tell mother I have had my Photograph taken and as soon as finished I will send one

Fitz Hugh Lee is reported as taken prisoner but needs confirmation there is a Col. Lee prisoner in the City

We expect to hear some strong news in a few days until then good Bye Write soon and accept this from your Son

A Cook Myrick

Excerpt from a Letter from John S. Kidder of Laurens to the father of Delevan Bates (in *Subdued by the Sword* by James M. Greiner) May 8, 1863

At this point Kidder did not know with certainty that Bates had been taken prisoner and was in Libby Prison.—Editor

Dear Sir,

It is with a sad heart that I pen a few lines to you to inform you of the painful intelligence of your son Delavan Bates. He is among the missing of our regiment. We went into a hard fought battle three miles west of Fredricksburg on Sunday last about 5:00 P. M. We were compelled to retreat and Delavan came out with me and we were rallying the men to resume the fight. I cannot find anyone who saw him fall and I think he was wounded and taken prisoner. My 1st Lieutenant

Butts said he saw him limp as he was coming out of the woods so he may have been wounded in the leg. I have done all that I could (either) to find out where he is or whether anyone saw him but I am unable to learn anything concerning him. I will say that none feel more deeply his loss than I do as I have never met with a friend that I thought as much of as Delavan Bates.

Excerpt from the Diary of
Andrew Adrian Mather, Sheriff of Otsego County

June 12, 1863
... drove up 3 miles beyond Middlefield center and arrested Charles Pendell, a deserter.

Excerpt from a Letter from
Elijah Keith of Milford to his wife, Caroline
June 12, 1863

Dear Wife
you will excuse me for writing again today, for it is a long lonely day with me. I wrote yesterday that we were to march and we did start, but after going about two miles a counter order reached us and we returned to camp and I having the remains of a bad cold in my throat the heat and dust made me cough quite bad and the result is headache and soreness in my left side. I am excused from duty today and am taking medicine and Amos made me some water gruel and I hope to recover in a few days again today at ten and a half oclock the forces here were put in motion going to the same place where they started for yesterday we hear there is a large force of the enemy out near Blackwater and our army think it is best to give them battle our regiment never had to leave me behind till today. I keep on the bed the most of the time and when I keep still I feel quite comfortable. One poor fellow of the 26th Michigan lost his life last night by the accidental discharge of a pistol was shot through the body and died instantly their camp is about 60 rods from ours. There is a man tenting with us named Henry A Waters that used to tend the picker in the Union Factory, he left it about the same time you did he seems to know Wm Lake and all the people that lived around there at that time. I shall have to stop and rest it is about time for the mail to come with your letter. 4 oclock PM your letter of last

Sunday has come; it is a comfort to me to learn that my family are well, but your despairing notes do not give me that courage that a more hopeful tome would you ask me if I don't sometimes regret that I enlisted when I am not well I have fears that I am not as useful as I ought to be but I did it in good faith and think still that it was my duty and placed in the same circumstances with only the same light I had then I think I should do the same as before but with the experience I have had in soldiering I am satisfied that my constitution was too much impaired to stand all kinds of weather and laying on the ground nights and the food in hot weather is such as would make me sick if I could not get any other ...

Excerpt from a Letter from Amasa Cook Myrick of Gilbertsville to his Father June 21, 1863

Fort Bennett

Dear Father

At the time of my writing there is a battle being fought on the old Bull Run battleground or else very near there it may possibly be at Centreville in Virginia which is about thirty miles from here the cannonading can be very plainly heard here and also in the direction of Harpers Ferry or in Loudon County Va. and it may possibly be another cavalry fight in "My Maryland." The first named battle is being fought between Generals Lee and Hooker they have been watching one another for several days past, and it was expected there would be a battle before this between these two Generals. "General Ewell" had the centre "Hill" the right and "Longstreet" the left of the rebels line, and near Thourofare Gap in the Blue Ridge, while Hookers headquarters are at Centreville or at least where Centreville once stood one log house some barracks and some ruins mark the place and forts loom up in every direction around there as well as here most if not all of the army of the Potomac and that of Lee's will be in this fight And I can do no other than hope that Hooker will come off victorious with the trapping and surrendering of Lee's whole Army This and the fall of doomed Vicksburg will I think end this terrible war

But how are the Butternuts braves getting along I hear verbally that they are armed with the Springfield rifle and are attached to the 41st militia I hope they will come to the aid of Pennsylvania for six months this is glorious weather for them Tell them not to hang back like a parcel of cowards but follow the example set before them in sixty one when we come. If it is bounty they are waiting for, shame on the cowards it will show at once they have not love enough for the "Glorious old Union" to come and fight for it in this her hour of need they lack that patriotism which every one now left there should have, and be the more ready for such emergencies of this kind than ever before every man or boy capable of bearing arms should enroll themselves as minute men ready at all times and for anything. I hear that Root is captain and Braily (?) & Donaldson Lieuts. & Caleb Sargt. Say is it so. Where is their Armory.

The news from Vicksburg is encouraging more and more every day. I hope that Grant will bring John (?) Pemberton to surrendering his troops and city to the Union and I think it will be done before long. The rebels there are getting more and more dissatisfied because Pemberton does not surrender and hundreds officers and men desert every day each one telling about the same story no pay and quarters rations A regiment the other day threw down their arms and cried we surrender we surrender but were forced to take them up again by being surrounded by a brigade these men will certainly desert if they can get a chance and come to our lines We have had some rain lately and it does not come amiss even to the Soldiers who like to see rain once in a while it has been intensely hot for a few days past but is now cooler it is raining now [there was] an Inspections this morning we were reviewed by General Barry last week and won the praise and admiration of the General.

Your Son, A Cook Myrick

Letter from Cyrus J. Hardaway of Pittsfield to his Mother July 5, 1863

I shall write to May Nelson as soon as it is light enough

On the Battle Field near Gettysburg

Dear Mother

I have been through one more terrible battle and thank God I am still safe and sound. But not so with the rest of my companions. Smith Haight is dead and Edwin Nelson is I am afraid mortally wounded. Also our captain is dead. James Reed is a prisoner with one more of our company named Kipp from Milford. We brought Haight and Nelson off from the field more than a mile. Smith died before we got him to the hospital. We gave him a very deacent burial and had a chaplain to read the burial Service. That is a great deal better than I have seen done by thousands of others for the last two days. We have whipped the Rebels badly this time and have held the field every night, but I hope that I shall never be obliged to lay on another battle field as long as we have lain here. The burial parties have been at work faithfully all the while but have not got near all the dead buried yet. The Enemy has fallen back and we followed them up this morning at day light. We found Reed and our other men in a hospital taking care of the wounded.

Our loss has been very heavy in general officers and so it has with the rebels. The rebel Cavalry has captured our mail so we do not get any more right away. I can't write any more now it is getting so dark. The Enemy left the most of their small arms on the field I should think from the guns that are left. I will write more as soon as I can.

Your affectionate Son
CJ Hardaway

Excerpt from "War Reminiscences" by Delevan Bates (published in *The Otsego Republican*, October 25, 1895)

The grand success of the Army of the Potomac at Gettysburg in July [1863] made everybody happy, but the New York riots called the 152d regiment to that city in place of the front, where all desired to go. About the middle of July the regiment reached the metropolis, where Gov. Seymour's "friends" were making things a little lively for good square Union people. The colored orphan asylum had been burned. The New York Tribune building had been partially destroyed and only saved from utter destruction by heroic fighting of a detachment of police who knew their duty and dared perform it. Col O'Brien of the 155th New York Vols. had been detached from his command and was trampled to death by the devilish mob. A battery of Napoleon guns had been trained on the rioters about the time the 152d regiment marched up Broadway to Mulberry Street. This had convinced the mob that the troops, now steadily arriving. meant business, and warlike demonstrations were less frequent.

Excerpt from a Letter from
Elijah Keith of Milford to his wife, Caroline
July 17, 1863

New York

Dear Wife:

You may be as much surprised as I am to learn that we have come to our own State to fight the copperheads I wrote in my last that we expected to go to Frederick Md, we had such orders but were thought to be needed more at this point to assist the police of the city in quelling the riots that occur here almost daily.

Excerpt from the Diary of
Andrew Adrian Mather, Sheriff of Otsego County

Aug. 2, 1863

Had my house stoned by Coperheads last night, made them skedaddle, caught one John Leonard and arrested Jasah Dorn Burgh. Got both in jail.

Excerpt from "War Reminiscences" by Delevan Bates
(published in *The Otsego Republican*, October 25, 1895)

In August [1863] the 152d went up for a few days, having a picnic all the time and no particular danger. Now, comrades of the 152d, tell the truth; wasn't that just a jolly time? Thence back to New York City and camping in the midst of "plug uglies" of the old sixth ward, while the second attempt to enforce the draft was made the season of pleasure was continued. The regiment now had the freedom of the city and attended the places of amusement whenever inclined, and the same jolly good times were known as while up at Schenectady. But temptations were great while here. New York City is the centre of all kinds of speculation and cussedness. Today Wall Street is working the United States Treasury. Then, speculators were tampering with the United States soldier. The Count of New York paid three hundred dollars for a volunteer. If a broker could get one for a hundred dollars there was two hundred dollars profit. And if he could be helped to desert and re-enlist under another name, two hundred dollars more could be realized.

Letter from
Edwin O. Arnold to William Chapin of New Lisbon
Camp of the 121st Regt., N.Y.S.V., near New Baltimore
August 30, 1863

Friend Will

I will try this pleasant sabbath day to answer your letter which I received a few days since. It is a pleasant day here. We had Reville Breakfast call, surgeons call, police call Conard mounting xc xc as usual this morning and one hundred of our regiment has gone out on a raid and to catch guerrellas. They don't take any Rations. They calculate to get their living. They search every house they come to and take what they want. It is rather tough but if they will be secesh they must suffer the consequences. Will I would like to be there this pleasant morning and hear the old church bell ring as usual and I would like to be there to go to church with you. I think we would enjoy ourselves first rate don't you Will. We would go down again in the evening a horseback. I would ride old Blue. You know after meeting we would coax some of the girls to let us see them safe home wouldn't we. I recon we would Will. This has been a great lesson to me and if I ever live to go home I shall know how to enjoy life better I think. It would be a great enjoyment to me to set down to a table and eat what you would call a good meal of vituals and then to have a soft feather bead to sleep in when it come night. But a soldier can get used to most anything. They can sleep on the cold ground with water two inches deep and live a half dozen hard tacks a day and a little piece of salt and march thirty miles. For we had to do it when we went from Fredericksburg to Gettysburg but thank the lord we gained the day by enduring such hardships and I hope we shall never have to endure as much as we have endured. But there has been great changes since the first of July. Brighter days dawning and we are everywhere Victorious and I hope we will continue, so until this cursed Rebellion is crushed out and the Stars and Stripes moving triumphant over every State in America and I think the time is not far distant. I may not live to see that day but if I don't live to enjoy it I hope some one will. I would to have you send me your photograph if convenient and I will send you another of mine. Wash is tough and hearty as ever and says he is waiting patiently for the time to come when he can put his arm around his dear beloved Libby and kiss her rosy cheeks. I would like to be there hop time. Will we would have fun occasionally I recon but be good courage for I shall hoping to meet you soon. Well I can't think of much more at present only I am enjoying good health at present and hope this will find you enjoying the same. Give my love to all and write soon and write all the news.

This from your true friend
Edwin O. Arnold
of Dixie

Letter from Amasa Cook Myrick of Gilbertsville to his Father September 13, 1863

Fort Bennett

Dear Father

Your letter of Sept 6th was received in due time and I take the first opportunity of answering it. I was very glad to hear from you

I also received with the letter a list of the drafted men of our town the most that was drafted It hit a good many that I was glad to see and a few that I would like to see some others I can mention in their places Will many of them come

I will when the Provost Marshall has done hearing the men's excuses the list who have to come who are exempt who paid their three hundred and who furnished substitutes

I would like to see Will Myrick drafted first rate it would do him good to come down here for a while but I do not think John would let him come. I would like to know whether John was a copperhead or not. I would like to be there and congratulate some of the lucky ones and I would like to see them in Virginia and have a little talk with them. We have finished the hospital that I was at work on and I am now back to the company doing duty bye expect to go away again this week to build barracks for the regiment The weather is quite moderate now we have had a nice shower last night and I was on guard the wind blew very hard and I never saw the dust so thick in my life. I could not see more then ten rods at the farthest.

War news is pretty good at present but expect to hear of some better soon

From your affectionate Son
A Cook Myrick

Letter from Nathaniel Fenton of Pittsfield to Almira Fenton November 16, 1863

Virginia Near the Rapidan River

Dear Wife

I once more take my pen in hand to write a few lines to you as I have not had a letter from you since the one that you wrote the 20 of October I can tell you that it has been a long time to me it is so lonesome that I do not know what to do to day and so I thought I would write a few lines...I have wrote you three letter and have not got an answer yet but I hope that I shall before long I have borrowed all of the postage stamps that I can to send letters to you and of that I have sent I cannot get an answer yet I hope that it is not your fault if you have not got any letters from me for I have wrote as often as every week and sometimes oftener we are between the Rapidan and the Rappahannock river we are encamped in the woods where the rebels commenced their camp they has some very good shanties made of logs which we took to make our shanties now it is about 7 feet wide and 10 feet long with a fire place and door at one end and a bed at the other wide enough for two to sleep in we have plenty to eat not of hardtack pork and fresh beef three times a week and plenty of coffee but not enough sugar and I have not had any money to buy any thing with since I left New York and I think that is a long time to wait for a little money when a letter will come through in two days Louisa sent me one dollar of state money but it was of no use to me down here for they would not take it it must be United States money to go here Oh Almira my dear wife I do believe if you knew how lonesome I am that you would write oftener than you do I cannot write as often as I should for it is so that I cannot while on a march for after marching all day and have to sleep on the ground at night and have to write by the light of a fire I do not feel as if I could write and have to march from 10 to 30 miles a day with a gun and coutrements a knapsack over coat woolen blanket rubber blanket shelter tent and all that you want to eat in 11 days I get pretty tired just think of it how you would feel after such a march and then see if your can blame me for not writing the first day that we left Warrenton we marched 27 miles in 8 hours that was pretty tough I thought Now the 16 Dear Wife I thought that I would not write until I got some stamps but I cannot wait any longer so I must write we are under marching order yesterday morning there was some heavy firing in front of us the rebels attacked our picket and our men shelled so they left for supper I had some hardtack pounded put water to them and a little salt and made some pancakes it is a new style I made a ring that I will send to you and see if you can tell what it is made of I wish that you would send me a fine comb if you please for I cannot get them here you need not wait to know where to direct a letter direct it to Washington DC 152 Reg NYSV Co H and it will come to my company let if be where it will you must not put this ring in hot water a great while at a time I am not very well today so I am excused by the Doctor.

Excerpt from a letter from
Lansing B. Paine of New Lisbon to his sister, Fan
Camp of the 121st Regt NYV near Brandy Station
December 24, 1863

Dear Sister Fan

I wish you a merry Christmas. Capt. Cronkhite & myself have bought a Goose for tomorrow & we calculate to have a good dinner. I started from Riker's Island a week ago last Monday in the steamboat <u>Promethius</u>. Had three hundred volunteers on board bound for the Army of the Potomac & Department of Washington. The sea was not very rough but I felt somewhat seasick & one Lieutenant on board did not set up much during the voyage. We did not reach the Capital of the Nation till Friday night. I had a fine view of Mount Vernon as we sailed up the Potomac: I have had a chance to see considerable during my sixteen months of service but as far as battlefields are concerned am perfectly satisfied but still think that this rebellion must be put down by force of arms & am willing to share the dangers of the field a spell longer. I started from Washington to Brandy Station last Sunday & arrived in camp about seven o'clock. Our Regt has a splendid camp far superior to the camp at Oak Church. Our Brigade lies just beyond Hazel River. Col. Upton commands the Brigade. Lt. Col. Olcott has returned but is on Court Martial so that Emmet is in command of the Regiment. I found Co K & E all well for the Regt appears very healthy. Lieut. Johnson has been transferred to my Co. I am at present in command of the Co as Capt Cronkhite is in Court Martial: They are granting Leaves and furlough at present & Lieut Dan Jackson will have a chance to visit New Lisbon this winter. The boys are all very strong Union & was very glad that the Copperheads were defeated in New York. The house I inhabit is built up of logs a good fireplace then there is Virginia mud used for mortar to plaster up the cracks. Tent cloths cover the top & then we have a good door in front with a wooden latch. Then comes our bedstead made of poles covered with evergreen boughs & plenty of blankets. Our tent has a floor composed of plenty of boards from a Virginia residence & today Lieut. Johnson has made some flour paste & papered the inside with newspapers. You see we understand soldiering better this winter then we did last. All the men have log houses that we can walk right in without stooping & as two companies form a street our city is composed of five streets & then the men have policed the camp so thoroughly that it looks very neat. I think I shall enjoy myself full as well here as on Riker's Island for now I am to work for my own Regt & myself. Emmet has been before an examing board at Washington & can have the Lieut. Colonecy for a colored Regt if he desires it. Did you ever see a fellow go ahead as he has done in everything? If this war should last till 23rd August 1865 (121st term of service) he would be a Colonel that is of course admitting his life is spared. If I should stay till 1865 & come home a Capt. I would be perfectly satisfied. As long as I am in business I shall always strive to do my duty: Lieut. Burrel (Co A) & Lieut Ridway (Co K) have gone home on Leaves. They live in Herkimer Co.: I expect to spend my Christmas on guard but I shall have a good dinner. The last letter from home was dated 21st. Father was full of business & had hired a Mr. Simmons to work for. Wm Gregories wife had died; I guess I have written all the news. I am feeling first rate. Give my respects to Carroll & remember me as your brother

Lansing

Excerpt from the Diary of John Wright of Richfield
January 17, 1864

Oh! what a sabbath for a man to see. Fighting, cursing, swearing and card playing. It is sick'ning to behold. Rations scanty - Bread Soup & Coffee. A perfect bedlam at the table. Some of the Boys fell at the Sutler's shanty and stove in the windows. The officers placed a guard around it. Warm and pleasant. The ground mostly bare.

Letter from Amasa Cook Myrick of Gilbertsville to his Father April 18, 1864

Fort Bennett

Dear Father

Doubtless you will be surprised to hear from me again so soon but it is about some business connected with myself and the army or in other words I am after a commission which through your influence and other I shall mention and which I expect I will succeed. In the first place I wish you to go to James L. Gilbert and state the case to him and get him to assist you through his brother Benjamin do not let James put you off without a trial but I think it will be necessary yes almost sure to have the influence of Benjamin

This you may think foolish in me a private to try to get a commission but all my hopes are through home influence and if you are acquainted with the Governor it will help a good deal. Perhaps some of James Gilberts friends are connected with the State affairs and personally well known with the Governor and could get such a favor granted without much trouble. The influence of George Hollis is worth a great deal being in the position he is in Albany do not fail to counsel him perhaps he can do the favor with no trouble at all and get it for the asking. Perhaps Will Clark will inform you how his son John procured his commission and this will be to you a great help I do not know of anyone else that you can go to for help in this case now do not take this for a joke for I was never more in earnest in my life and I wish you to rush this matter through it must be done quick for there are over twenty vacancies in the Regt. And will be filled soon do not let Fred Howard know of anything of this and tell no one but those that are necessary under and circumstances because if I fail I do not wish it to get back here again. Jones and Ira Green with some others started for home today we were on a brigade review to day and passed [off well] I will now close hoping for success let me hear from you soon from your Son

A Cook Myrick

Letter from L. D. Fairchild of Exeter to his Wife
April 20, 1864

Port Corcoran

Dear Wife

Having a few moments to my self this morning just before fatigue time I have to go out this morning I thought I would improve it by writing you a few lines.

I was over to Washington yesterday and had a very pleasant time I visited most all of the publick buildings and almost all of the places of note in Washington I tell you that the publick buildings are splendid but take them away I think that it is about the meanest looking city that I ever was in as I told you in my letter before if it was not for the publick buildings it wold be no place at all.

I had my photographs taken I shall get them on Thursday then I shall send them right along there is no particular news now every thing is as usual over hear no war news I am satisfied that we shall have to stay here for they are making every thing for the health and comfort of the soldiers at the place

I send you a draft in this letter for twenty five dollars you can probably get Mr Branard to cash it or he will get it cash for you I shall send you some if they pay us the first of May I do not know wether they will or not we can't always tell when they will pay us if they do I will send it I send in this two photographs the colord soldiers is for Ally and the other for Eunice

There is two of Walter Wood brother in our regiment you recollect one that worked for Uncle Luman and a brother older they are in the Band they have played in it for the last two years I came across them Monday last at the general review so I will wish you good by this time I shall write this week again remember me to all enquiring friends and kiss the children for me and give them my love and keep a good share for yourself God Bless you all

This from your most Affectionate Husband
L. D. Fairchild

Excerpt from the Diary of Lansing B. Paine of New Lisbon

He was taken prisoner at the battle of The Wilderness, May 6, 1864.
—Editor

June 21, 1864 Sun.

A Roman Catholic priest came in to see us; he informed us that our men were dying off at a rate of fifty to seventy-five a day at Andersonville, Ga. Our government should be informed and do something about it.

Excerpt from the Diary of John Wright of Richfield
May 13, 1864

Great excitement. Co. L. was ordered out of the Bomb proof to make room for 200 Rebel Prisoners who are to be kept in close confinement. Co. L. goes in "A" tents. The war news is glorious. Grant is everywhere successful.

Excerpt from the Diary of John Wright of Richfield
May 18, 1864

Wake up and hear the cannon booming in the distance. 7 o'clock arrive on the field of Battle. May God support me. It is horrible to see the wounded. Was allowed to rest. Don't know how soon we may be called upon to move on the enemy. 9 A.M. the battle rages, it is reported that we are driving the enemy. 1:30 loaded for the first time. 7 P.M. have pitched tents for the night; but we are liable to be called out at any moment. The report is that the enemy are sorely pressed.

Letter from Amasa Cook Myrick of Gilbertsville to his Father
June 6, 1864

Camp in the Field near Gaines Mills & Hill

Dear Father

It has been some time since I have written to you and for good reasons. We have been marching and fighting every day but two since we joined the Army of the "Potomac" we belong to the fighting 2nd

Corps commanded by Genl "Hancock" and fighting 1st Division commanded by Genl. "Barlow" and 1st Brigade commanded by Col. Miles of the 61st N. Y. & a fighting brigade it is the Regt. Has lost severely since we started. We were relieved from the extreme front last night and are now resting a little but will not last long I fear we have had in our company killed 7 wounded 17. Capt. Klinck was among the wounded Lieut. Kenyon who used to be in our company is killed Lieut. Williamson & Lieut. Fred Howard who were in our company have each lost a leg and it is feared Fred will lose his life. We have marched night and day fought and worked night and day nearly all the time. I suppose you have watched the papers and seen partial lists of casualties most all that are wounded are in the leg some in other parts of the arm and body of all stories of the horrors of war and the battle field you have heard or read have never been exaggerated and I never should believe it myself if I had not seen it with my own eyes. We are within 6 or 8 miles of Richmond on the Peninsula and will have to fight every inch of the way there and we are going there this time sure every one is confidant of success. I have not had a scratch yet and have been in the thickest of the fight a bullet went through my pants at the battle of the Pines we have been in three General engagements and under fire and skirmishes almost every day. Part of our company were on picket one day and charged and captured the Johnnys first line of works we captured 34 prisoners in that charge the wounded that you know from our company are T. H. Musson G. Austin, Gus Green, G. Graves, J. Caulkin, R. Slade, Wm. Alsop No one killed the boys are generally well some were left behind when we started the regt numbers between 12 & 1300 in all we started with 1 less than 1900. This is heavy artillery in earnest. I think we will have a siege train in a few days but am not certain and I hope we will then pay the Johnnys our compliments to a better advantage and one we are more used to than the rifle but we can use either. I have seen the boys of the 152nd and 121st several times. Things are going along as fast as possible we have had very beautiful weather most of the time

But no more this time write soon we have received no mail since we started my respects to all endearing friends
Direct to A Cook Myrick
Co E 2nd N. Y. V. Arty Washington D. C.

Excerpt from the Town of Otsego Records
June 10, 1864

At a special town meeting held at the Court House in the village of Cooperstown in and for the town of Otsego in pursuance of a call previously made and posted according to law Horace M Hooker was duly Elected chairman of Said meeting.

On motion of E Countryman, George W Ernst, E M Harris, Hezekiah Sturgess, James Hendryx, J K Leaning were duly elected a war committee for the town of Otsego. The following resolutions were duly passed and adopted by said meeting.

Resolved that the town of Otsego pay each of the veterans who re-enlisted for the town of Otsego and who have been credited to the town under a previous call of the President, a bounty of three hundred dollars and that the town issue bonds. The following resolution was duly passed and adopted by said meeting Resolved that the town pay the bounty or bond due to Robert Burk, to his family and that the same be used for the future benefit of his family and for their Education and support hereafter and not to pay his old debts. The meeting then adjourned.

John E. Brown Town Clerk

Excerpt from "War Reminiscences" by Delevan Bates (published in *The Otsego Republican*, October 25, 1895)

Bates is discussing the charge on the Weldon Railroad.—Editor.

The cavalry struck the road and did considerable damage, but the infantry, after striking the [Weldon] railroad, struck a rebel corps under A. P. Hill, and the 152d Vols. had the pleasure of meeting Mahone's brigade of Virginians, the same that the colored troops met a few weeks later at the battle of the Mine. I think this was the worst day the regiment ever saw on the battlefield. The skirmish line under Captain Hensler was captured, and when the rebel line reached the regiment things got awfully mixed. The firing was so rapid and the confusion so great that every man used his own judgment, some going in one direction and some in another. Captain Burt, who was in command, reached the plank road with the flag and rallied the remnant of the regiment in as good shape as could be expected under the circumstances. Much better than did several other regiments which were totally broken up and captured with their colors. The Confederates captured about twenty-five hundred of the 2d corps and several hundred more from the 6th corps in this engagement. The 152d lost forty-nine men and four officers. Captain Hensler, Captain Gilbert and Lieutenant Campbell were taken prisoners. The regiment for the next three weeks was kept steadily at work night and day building breastworks, cutting down timber, making abattis and clearing out roads.

Excerpt from a Letter from Samuel D. French to his Sister July 5, 1864

I would have been as glad to spend the 4th with you as you to have me but of course we cannot always have things as we like so we must content ourselves with taking the world as we find it. As you say time passes very swiftly and if nothing happens to prevent we will have a chance to have a good long visit in a little more than a year. Sure I am in a sort of bondage now but it was voluntary on my part so I have no business to grumble. I would do the same thing again under the same circumstances. Don't you think I am getting to be a Virginian in grand Style. I have got a <u>Cullared Jemimen</u> for a cook. We are on his Master's plantation from which he ran away when he heard the <u>Yanks</u> were crossing the James river. He would like to have the Army move so he could get away from home. he thinks he has lived here long enough. Of course we live high. Hard Bread. Salt pork. Coffee & Sugar is our "Bill of fare" with fresh beef occasionally. Yesterday morning I got 20 lbs beef Steak for the 10 of us but it is all gone now. I presume we will get some vegetables soon as the Sanitary Commission is to furnish the troops with them.

Excerpt from *The Freeman's Journal,* July 8, 1864

The Ladies of Cooperstown will give a Fair for the benefit of our sick and wounded soldiers, in Judge Nelson's new brick block, corner of Chestnut and Main streets - on Thursday, July 21st. the opening will begin at 12. Those who desire Ice Cream for dinner can be provided for. The Fair will continue from 12 to 11 P. M. It is earnestly desired that there be a large attendance.

The Fair for the Soldiers to be held on the 21st of this month, should not be forgotten. We are requested to hint to some of our liberal hearted farmers that a few pounds of live geese feathers would be thankfully received, to be made up in cushions for wounded men. They may be left with Miss Pickens.

Excerpt from *The Freeman's Journal*, July 29, 1864

The Fair for the Soldiers held in this village [Cooperstown] last week, was a decided success. The ladies interested in it took hold energetically and accomplished a great deal of work in a short time. Several articles of value, contributed by different person, were disposed of by a lot, and helped materially to swell receipts. The contributions for the ice cream and refreshment room were on a liberal scale, and that department of the fair netted a very handsome sum. The rooms in Judge Nelson's new building, where the fair was held, were handsomely trimmed with flags, evergreens and flowers, reflecting the good taste of the young ladies who did the work. The attendance was so large on Thursday evening, that many persons were unable to gain admittance. The aggregate receipts amounted to about $695 Disbursements for general expenses, material made up, &c., $138 – net proceeds $557. A draft for $527 was sent the President of the Christian Commission, and $30 sent the Sanitary Commission for the purchase of material to be made for the soldiers.

In this connection we publish the following extract from an officer's letter, dated Near Petersburg, July 13:

"The weather continues intensely hot. We have had no rain now for more than 50 days, and the dust, as our trains move, is actually suffocating. Our poor soldiers in the trenches suffer beyond description; but they all stand up under it bravely, and the entire army is in good spirits and confident of ultimate success. They all complain, however, of not being paid. There is now more than four months' pay due them; but the officers are worse off then the men. The soldiers are all well fed and clothed, but the poor officers have to find themselves. The Sanitary Commission is an institution a credit to every one who has helped them. They have their stores in the wagons here at the front, and wagons passing from City Point to all parts of the army. They keep the soldiers supplied with vegetables, the hospitals with delicacies, &c. The Christian Commission is also another good Samaritan affair."

Lieut. F. W. Foot, of the 121st Regt., reported killed, is alive and a prisoner in Libby Prison Hospital, Richmond. He was wounded in an engagement on the 10th of May, captured, and was obliged to have a leg amputated above the knee.

Excerpt from a Letter
Elijah Keith of Milford to his wife, Caroline
August 20, 1864

… the question is whether my furlough will be granted any the sooner for my improved health or be a good reason for delaying it in order to give sick and wounded men a chance. I am glad to receive the blessing of <u>partial</u> recovery even at the expense of my furlough. I doubt not but that will come, in reasonable time, and that time I am perfectly willing to wait, everyday now counts on toward the end of my second year, and then comes the third and last, and I hope and pray it may prove the last year of the rebellion but I dare not pray even for the war to stop as long as there are any armed rebels fighting against our government. I do not see why people need to be discouraged everything is progressing finely and success will be sure to attend our efforts if we put them forth in a proper manner trusting in God but if we have become convinced that we are in the right and our cause is not just and therefore not approved of God we do well to be discouraged and the best thing we can do is to petition the next Congress to offer the "Southern brethren" "liberal terms of peace" and confess our faults and ask their pardon; but if we are in the right and our cause that of justice and God and humanity I see no way to dodge responsibility without incurring the displeasure of God and the contempt of the whole civilized world. I greatly fear that the copperhead "leaven" is at work among the people at home the fainthearted are beginning to look on the muddy raging waters of strife and shrink from the perilous task of walking on the water and consequently begin to sink let all such look to God, as Peter did, and not turn away from Him by seeking relief from wicked designing men who from the beginning of this war have opposed nearly every measure proposed to carry it forward and now would fain have us believe that if <u>they</u> could only get the lines into their hands they would soon drive into the part of peace, but such a peace as would make every honest man blush to think himself a man …

Letter from
John E. Hetherington of Cherry Valley to H. C. Garrison
September 8, 1864

Captain,

I have the honor to transmit herewith a Surgeon's Certificate of disability.

I have been sick abed for the past week and unable to do the business or I should have sent them sooner. I tendered my Resignation most two weeks since but have heard nothing from it. <u>Give my Best Regards to the Officers of the Regt.</u>

Very Respectfully,
J. E. Hetherington

Letter from Charles H. Gould to his Parents
October 6, 1864

Dear Parents,

Here I am at City Point. I arrived here yesterday P.M. and have been sick like a dog ever since I left Syracuse, sleeping on the ground every night, and rations too bad to tell & among 800 substitutes, started from Elmira Saturday P. M., arrived at Baltimore by rail and then got aboard the vessel, sailed down through Chesapeake Bay, up through Hampton's Roads, entering in the James river and coming here. Among the 800, all jumped the bounty hit about 130. You can't answer this readily.

<u>Barber</u> is to <u>pay</u> by the seventh of this month. Be sure and have everything right in regard to the house.

Say nothing to Hattie about the times I have. Look on the map and find City Point. There you can see where I am. I am writing about 6 o'clock in the morning. It is very hot here, very hot indeed. It was as hot yesterday P. M. as it was in New York State last summer. We are behind fortifications all right. I have seen great sights so far. I will write as quick as I get to my destination. Please tell Hattie the same. I shall write as quick as I possibly can. From you son,

Chas. H. Gould

I got my destination. I spoke to the Captain, Provost Marshall yesterday and he thought he would take me from the (Subs) today and have me a reporter from the army. Just think of me within six miles where the worst fighting is going on, now since the rebellion. I wrote Hattie the first day I arrived at Elmira, and I can't write her again or you. I don't know when, so let Ellie write her for me, 142 West Thirty-first st. New York (Hattie G. Bowens) Tell her I shall write as quick as I can, and give her a good letter. We lived on bread and raw salt pork, and hardly a drink of water from the time we left Baltimore until we arrived here. The water being salt until we get up the James a great ways. I am now up more than the rest of the boys. Only, the Capt. P. M. does something for me. Just warn all of the folks never, never to go to war. I see enough of this first day I left Syracuse. They played it on me. It was all right while I was at Syracuse, but after you once leave from there they have nothing to do with you. Be sure and get a receipt for the $1000, that rec'vd.

Letter from Charles H. Gould to his Parents
Camp near Petersburg
October 12, 1864

I am at my destination: One and one half miles from Petersburg. I can see, by going a short distance, Petersburg quite plain, hear the firing of cannons and muskets, seeing the bursting of shells and other things too numerous to mention. I am in "Co. D, United States first Sharp Shooters," or Berdan's 1st S.S. Write quick and direct as follows: ("Chas. H. Gould, Co. D, 1st U.S.S.S.") Every moment and every other fifth second, I can hear the bursting of shells, or by turning around see them burst in the air. It is about 7 o'clock in the evening. I am in Lt. Hodgson's camp, I am assisting him in writing, and shall for a time to come. I left City Point yesterday. Coming along I had the pleasure of seeing Gen. Hancock! Gen. Grant!! and other great men of the day. I saw while at City Point, a Negro shoot a white man. The negro being stationed "on guard" front of the "guard house" to keep persons from there and let no one out. It was an old man. The negro says, "Put down dat window! Put down that window or I shoot," and the next thing I saw, he discharged his gun at him, taking effect in the heart, killing him instantly. The old man, as it appears hoisted the window easily and came to put it down. It was hard, and could not get it down quick enough, so the miserable thing shout. He was "Court Martialed," and shot today.

I referred how the officers, that accompanied us from Elmira to City Point - in my last - used us, was every one put under arrest, "Court

Martialed" and some were discharged while others were sent to hard labor for six months.

I am quite contented, I am in the same regiment George Tuckerman, Wm. McLean, Chas. McLean, Hetheringtons, and all of the boys from Cherry Valley. There being only 8 companies left out of the 10, and their time will all expire by next spring at the last. Then I will, I expect, be transferred to the 2nd U.S.S.S. We have a splendid rifle to shoot with. I am in the 1st Camp and had an opportunity of looking over the list of this Reg't. and seeing all of the names of our boys from Cherry Valley. Seeing the names of those that was dead and living. Did you write to Hattie, as I told you, if you did not, I want you to do it without fail. I shall write tomorrow to her. Tell her where to direct, and then I will receive the letters. It is quiet before Petersburg at present, only "picket firing" and cannonading from one battery to another. The Johnny's (rebels I mean) come across every day, telling the same. "The rebels can't stand it much longer." The Lt. - I am a fine fellow. He knew all of the C. V. boys. You can send the letter to J. R. Dixon, and don't fail. Tell everyone to write to me. Each Brigade is favored with a "band of music" and sitting as I am now, hearing the guns thundering and muskets roaring with the band sending forth its onward march, it makes one feel quite "romantic" here.

I forgot myself, don't send this letter away, because I have spoken of one that is so <u>dear</u> to me. Let no one out of the family see it. See to the payment of the house, that Barber is to pay. Get a receipt. Be sure and get the rent of our house. If he runs over a month, make him leave and you occupy it. I have seen enough already, that I would not exchange for the money I received. I spoke rather discouraging in my last of the army. It is pleasant when you once arrive at your regiment. Wm., give my respect to Geo. Brassert (?) I will stop and bid you good night, and all my love, (except what belongs to another) to you all, and have a chat with the Lt.

Your aff. And obedient Son,
Chas.

Letter from Robert B. Davidson to his Father
October 18, 1864

Bay Point, S. C.

Dear Father

I now sit down to write a few lines to you in answer to your welcome letter I received some time ago but delayed answering it for we were expected to get Payed every day but we have not got any Pay yet and they tell us we are not going to get pay in a Month yet then we will get four Months Pay the recruts have got here we got twenty Eight in our Company but they are playing the duce with the Company for there is four or five Coperheads amongst them they stick up for McClelen and there is a fight almost every day but we got them pretty well Cooled down when we get talking on Politicks they Sneek off like a Dog that has been killing Shepp they have no peace night or day we call them all the traters and every thing we Can to provolk them one fellow swor he Could fech Mc men enough out of the recruts to which all the old Company so we steped out and there was more recruts for the old fellows then there was for him so he has kept pretty still ever since but old Abe will get all the Old Soldiers voats and most of the Navey but there is a great maney Mc men in the Navey but I think old Abe is shure enough to be elected we have all got our voating papers made out but we have not got the tickets yet I send mine to you it will make the Coperheads stare some when they see the big invelop come up to the balet we have been working pretty hard for some time the Navey has got posesion of this Island and we have been removinig the Cannon and all the government stors across the river the talk is that we are going into a fort on the other side of the river we stand a pretty good chance for we have got our name up in the ordinance Department of keeping the fort in the best order of any fort in the Department but I must close this leaves me and all the rest of the Glorie boys well hopeing this will find you all the same write soon Direct as before may live to see you all from your Son
Robert B. Davidson

Petter Penny is at
N'york he is in the
Invlid Corps
He is pretty Smart again

Excerpt from the Diary of John Wright of Richfield
October 21, 1864

Weak, Weak, Weak. No very severe pain except in chest when I have to cough. Diarreah keeps me to about <u>the same</u> degree of weakness.

Excerpt from the Diary of John Wright of Richfield
October 25, 1864

John W. Wright departed this life on Tuesday, Oct. 25, 1864 in hospital in the military prison at Salisbury, N.C.
   A. Young

Excerpt from *The Freeman's Journal*, October 28, 1864

In anticipation for an early call for men from this State, especially should Lincoln be re-elected, it would be well for the Board of Supervisors at its approaching session to make provision for raising at least half a Million of Dollars, by taxation and a moderate use of bonds, to be used for paying bounties to volunteers. Unless something of this kind is done, towns will again be found bidding against each other, and bounties will be run to a very high figure for one year men.

The hardships of the draft have been greatly increased by the recent decision announced last week, in the following paragraph: -

"Many of the men recently drafted here, have run off or hid themselves. In view of this fact, enquiries were recently addressed to the Provost Marshall, who replied, that drafted men who fail to report and do not actually enter the service, are not credited on the quota. A supplementary draft will be made for and deficiencies that may exist after the present draft is completed.

The practical effect is this: A town has 100 men who are liable to the draft, and 25 is the quota; of this number 15 or 20 "run off" when drafted; they are situated so that they can leave; others are not; and they must run two or three chances of being drafted – to fill the places of deserters on the army! This decision will have the effect intended by Mr. Fry – but is it fair and just?

Excerpt from *The Freeman's Journal*, November 11, 1864

An incident or two occurred at the polls in this village, on Tuesday last, which doubtless had their counterpart elsewhere. Jacob and John Blonck are legal voters of this town and election district - their names being duly registered. They enlisted in the army during the present year, and are now in the service. They sent on the specified proxies, with their vote, directed to J. F. Scott. Esq., who does business in this town, but lives just over the line in Middlefield. There was no question as to their being voters, or as to their signatures, the only point - raised by several Republicans present - was that the votes were not sent to an elector of this town, and hence, under a strict construction of the law, should not be received. It was insisted, on the other side, that these were good and true votes, that there was no fraud intended or charged, and that a liberal and just construction of the law would allow of their being received. Mr. Bowen, Chairman of the Board of Inspectors, so held; but his Republican associate was decidedly opposed to it, and the other Democratic member said that a strict and literal construction of the law would compel him to decide the same way - though he knew the Blonks to be legal voters of this district. This is a hard case, as all must admit. We shall not complain of the action of the Board; yet we do not believe these votes should be lost to the brave men who sought to cast them for the candidates of their choice.

The law is one which, with the experience of this election before them, men of both parties will be willing to see materially amended.

Letter from Thomas Smith to L. W. Rathbun of Middlefield
Camp near Park Station, Virginia
November 15, 1864

Dear Sir it is with plasure that I sit down to let you know how I am getting along my health is very good at present and hope it is all well with you and all the friends there is nothing going on here more than picket firing and that the keep up more nights that the do day time but my right arm is lame yet with the way the boys check it when I got here the Regiment is very small and only four company in all we can see the rebbel and talk with them good many of them keep coming in every day and give them selves up this is a hard looking country you cant see anyting but pine woods and mud holes all the women that I seen here has beard on like a man so you see there will be no danger of falling in love with them the all say that the are sick of the War Burnside is nigers has a fine time in picket the keep firing all the time the picket line is not more than 50 yards a part the 5 corps tore up about 25 miles of the branch that run from the Waldon to the south side road with out much of a fight we have a very strong breast works in front of us here but I dont think the will attack this plase if the do the will go back with Sore heads Gen Right is here in command I have not been on picket yet but to morrow will be our turn to go but we dont never know much trouble when we go on picket we dont fire in less the fire first but the dont like the nigers in one plase the are so close each other that when we ask them for some tobacco that they through it a cross from one line to the other tell Kate that I like it here better than I did at Chester hospital the time pases a way quicker then it did when I was there but this is a low swampy plase it was very cold when I came here but now the weather is warm and plasant I con not think of any thing more to write this time you must write and let me know how you all get a long

Yours truly
Thomas Smith

Letter from L. D. Fairchild of Exeter to his Wife November 20, 1864

City Point

Dearest Wife

I received your kind letter to day and was very glad to hear from you once more I have received your letters eather on a Thursday or Friday night before but some how or other it passed by this time I begin to think I should loose it all to gether so now I am all right again I still continue to enjoy good health hoping that these few lines will find you all enjoying the best of God blessings that is good health and liberty there is not any particular news at this time every thing appears to be still it has ben raining for two or three days back and is raining now it will probably make the roads impassable if it does there will be nothing done for a spell at any rate there has ben a rumor that our corps was going to relieve the 19th corps they are with Sheridan and some says that they are going down to North Carolina wich one it will be I can't say I don't believe as yet eather you said that Milton West had sent home my blanket I am glad of it I had some shirts in the same box you did not say wether they come or not wether I put my woolen gloves in with the rest or not I can not say or wether I throwd them away with my other things on the march if I did and you have got them I wish you wold do them up in a good package and sent them by mail to me we have it very cold here by spells I think they will come safe enough at any rate I wold risk it that is if you have got them I suppose that you have it very hard in making up your mind about what you want the most every thing is so high the only way that I can recommend is to get what you really need the most I am in hopes to send you some more money before long I was in hopes that they wold of paid us when our two months was due but they have not and now I suppose they won't until January that will close up the year I am glad that you have Charlie some flannel I hope you will be able to get the rest some to or something else as warm you think that every thing is high at home I grant it is but it don't commence with this place you have to pay from twelve to fifteen dollars for a pair of boots and nothing extra at that and for a vest from ten to twelve dollars and every thing else in proportion butter 80 cents per pound so on down to the smallest thing it is four times as high as it is in any other place I don't know that I have any thing more to write at this time if Milton is at home yet I wish he wold write to me and let me know when he is going to stop when he comes back if he is gone try and find out where is gone to I am still in my place yet and I am going to stay this time as long as I can give my love to the children and kiss them give my love to all enquiring friends and keep the biggest share for yourself God bless you and keep you all in good health until my return again

This from your most
Affectionate Husband
L. D. Fairchild

Excerpt from *The Freeman's Journal*, December 9, 1864

An appeal has been made in behalf of the Southern Union Refugees, thousands of whom are in great distress and the most abject poverty. Women and children are severe sufferers. Articles of cast-off clothing as well as money, will be received and forwarded by Miss Susan F. Cooper. What you feel inclined to do in that direction, do as soon as convenient.

Letter from S. Gordon to John Marsh
December 14, 1864

Norwich Headquarters

John Marsh
Enrolling Officer [of Otsego County]

Sir

I am in the receipt of your communication Dec. 12, 1864 accompanied with Surgeons Certificate &c. Mr Weaver must report and be examined by the Board before his name will be stricken from the roll. So of all other persons in like category. The Board is in continuous Session day by day to hear all such cases.

No Surgeon not appointed by the Government will be allowed to exercise the functions of the Board including its Surgeon and superceded its jurisdiction. The impropriety will strike you forcibly on a moments reflection.

Cases of manifest permanent Physical Disability such as entire loss of teeth on either jaw, Club feet, loss of leg, one foot, hand &c should not be enrolled. You ought by this time to know what is meant by permanent physical disability. A natural born fool, a confirmed lunatic, a person on his dying bed in the last stages of consumption and many other cases that might be enumerated as coming within the definition of manifest permanent disability.

The application of common sense will solve all difficulties involved in any case that may come under your official action as Enrolling Officer.

Respectfully &c
S. Gordon
Capt & Pro[vost] Mar[shal]
19th Dist NY

Excerpt from *The Morris Chronicle*, July 6, 1904

John N. Daniels describes Andersonville Prison as it was in 1864.—Editor.

... a little back from the southeast corner ... was located what we were told was the prison hospital of which nothing but the tops of the tents could be seen from the inside. What really existed in this direction outside the prison I am unable to say from personal knowledge, never having visited it.

Northeast and south the country was a blank to us, with the exception of a small portion of the valley through which the stream continued eastward; this was very meager, terminating in a wooded swamp ten or fifteen rods from the stockade.

We may trace the road from its point of entering into view down toward the north gate. It is the way over which nearly 13,000 poor fellows passed never to return. Their deliverance was by the south gate, where they were loaded in a mule wagon and driven to their silent home in the cemetery by an old colored man, and delivered to a company of our own men under parole for burial, which, as there was plenty of time and help, was done in a respectable manner.

A trench six foot in width and long enough to hold the bodies of each day's mortality was dug in which they were placed side by side, their identity preserved by a piece of board bearing the number corresponding to the name, company and regiment of the deceased kept in the prison register.

I was in the vicinity of the burial place on several occasions. The graves were in long, straight and perfect rows, neatly rounded mounds with its board markers indicating each one. The government has purchased here fifty acres of surrounding land, including the cemetery, and has replaced the board markers with neat stone tablets, and beautified the grounds with shrubs and evergreens. A resident keeper is in charge who conducts relatives or friends visiting the cemetery to the

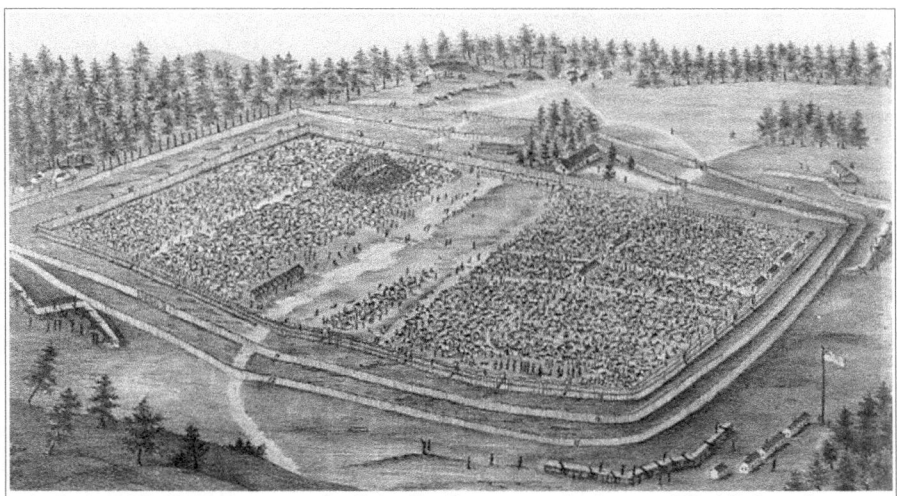

Andersonville Prison as seen by John L. Ransom, Author and Publisher of "Andersonville Diary, Escape and List of the Dead," Washington, D.C., A. Sachse & Co., c1882.

resting place of the lost loved one if he be not of the unknown, of whom there are 400 resting there whose markers bear simply this significant inscription, "unknown." Significant is this that they had no friend in the prison when sickness and suffering came upon them to minister unto them in the physical want, in the cheering comforting word to hear, and to bear the dying message to distant dear ones. Significant again in that in a strange land alone they have and must ever rest in graves over which the flowers of affection have never been strewn the tears of loving remembrance never shed. They gave themselves to their country and to their country alone they belong.

As we resume our interrupted way along the road to the prison entrance, the same objects meet our view as on our first entrance. I think the first buildings we approach are occupied by the teamsters. Those nearest the stockade are the cooking establishments.

... the roadway did not extend across the stockade, but only half or two thirds the way, the remaining distance was given up to the prisoners. Again the descent to the stream is more abrupt then we would suppose from appearances ... and of greater extent. The slope was most gradual on the south side and extended clear back to the stockade on the north side. Although the assent continued clear back to the line, the abruptness terminated in about half the distance, the latter portion being very gradual, but little rising above the level. I should think the extreme elevation on either side above the level of the stream must have been nearly 100 feet.

We note the bridge near the deadline on the western side where the stream enters the prison. The varying course, bordering morass, the larger portion of which lay on the northern side.

Dimly against the northern wall of the stockade can be seen the barracks or receiving hospital...Our friends found shelter in the last one but one to the right. In the southeast corner can be seen four other buildings, these were to have been devoted to the same purpose, I think but were only completed at about the time the camp was broken up, so were of brief if any use.

Directly beneath our point of observation over the southeast corner of the prison, we see a portion of the new hospital. This was not ready for use until shortly before the evacuation. The old hospital is back and not shown in [the] picture.

I think this must conclude the best explanation I am able to give of the place and locality. Those who had friends or relatives in the prison should be able to know approximately the place they occupied, to mark the course of their approach, and the objects of interest with which they had to do and with which they were surrounded. Those who shared the imprisonment may identify the old familiar places, and all I trust who have interest in history of this hell of suffering may become more familiar with it.

Excerpt from a Letter from Lewis M. Bryant of Butternuts, published in *The Otsego Republican*, January 6, 1865

I belong to the Second N. Y. Heavy Artillery. I was taken prisoner near Bottoms Bridge, Va., June 13th, 1864. We were marched to Richmond, Va., robbed of our money, blankets and most of our clothes and confined in Libby prison for eight days. Nothing occurred here worthy of note. We were crowded into a large room and lived on corn bread and water. The air being foul and almost suffocating, I, on one occasion, put my face to a grated window for relief, and was fired at by the guard outside, the ball just grazing my ear. I then learned that a breath of air at that window had cost many a poor boy his life.

On the 28th we arrived at Andersonville. The prison is a field of twenty-five acres, mostly wet, marshy ground, surrounded by a fence or stockade as it is called, built up of square timbers, close and tight, about twenty feet high. We found in it thirty-thousand prisoners - the addition of our company making thirty-eight thousand. As we entered this place of cruelty, starvation and death, I shall never forget the heart-sickening picture that presented itself as I cast my eyes over the twenty-five acres of filthy, ragged, naked, lousy, sick and starving mass of still living human skeletons. Thousands were without hat or shoe; many without coat, vest or shirt, and others as naked as Adam before the fall. Some were shouting, some praying, some cursing, some crying for food, some weeping, and some whose suffering had crazed the brain were fighting their comrades and giving orders for battle, under the supposition that they were charging on the rebel army.

As we entered the broad gate and looked upon this horrid scene, a companion of mine, heart-sickened and trembling in every limb, looking up to me with tearful eyes, and voice choking with emotion, asked (in the language of a poem I have since seen) "for God's sake, Bryant, is this hell?"

Negroes were kept constantly at work digging trenches in which to bury our dead. After we had deposited them in piles outside the gate, they were thrown by the rebels and negroes into a large, six-mule wagon, carted by loads to the trenches, thrown in amid the scoffs and jeers of the rebels, without regard even to *decency*, and left to sleep till the great day of final accounts. As I have said before, all the men were filthy, ragged or naked, and swarmed with vermin. The limbs of many were palsied and stiff with scurvy. Some of them were swollen by dropsey almost to bursting. Thousands were seen whose bones pierced through the tightly drawn flesh - reduced by starvation - and sores formed at the hips, shoulderblades, etc., were filled with slimy maggots, whose every motion was untold agony to the unhappy sufferers who had not the strength to remove them. No care was taken of these martyrs, no medicine given, no attempt made to relieve them. They died by hundreds, to be buried like brutes. And all because they loved their country and fought for their flag. It is believed by the prisoners and sometimes admitted by our guard to be the policy of rebels, to starve in prisons those that they cannot kill upon the field - that such as do not die in their hands shall be so entirely broken down as not to be able again to lift their muskets against them. And it will never be better until the southern confederacy experiences religion, or our government adopt the system of retaliation - two things not likely to occur.

I am not an educated man nor skilled with the pen, but if I were, and understood *all* languages, I could not half express the sufferings of the prisoners in Georgia. And if the devil does not have the authors of their misery, I really cannot see the use of having any devil at all.

Very truly yours,
Lewis M. Bryant

Excerpt from *The Freeman's Journal*, January 13, 1865

We are happy to announce the escape of Lieut. Morris Foot, of this place (Cooperstown), from a rebel prison in Georgia, and his return home. He was on Gen. Wessell's Staff, at Portsmouth, at the time of his capture.

Letter from Charles B. West to Peter Chapin of New Lisbon January 22, 1865

Camp New Petersburgh Va

Friend Peter

I now beg leave to write a few lines to you to let you know that I am well and enjoying life well for a Soldier and it is my wishes that these few lines finds the old farmer enjoying life although it is hard times to enjoy life in these war times and it is hard to fight under such a d__m nigger administration but it is but a short time that this old regt has to serve it is warm here there is not any snow but a concitable rain there is not much news here at presant we have just had a neat little victory at willmington the capture of fort fisher that will put an end to the blockading there for the presant the news here is that they are leaving petersburgh but this is a decerters story but they all tell me story about it there is quite a number of Johnny come in every night the other night there was a Brigadear General and a curnel come over on the lord side they all say that there cause is hopeless and that they are sick of this long and bloody war Well it is enough to make a mans blood run cold but it must be done if a man should tell what he has seen at home they would say that is a yarn but if they should be here and see one Battle field after the fight and the wounded at the Hosptails he would say God forbid such hostilitys pleas answer this give me all the news a so forth With these remarks i close

I remain your Friend
B. West

Oneonta Monument

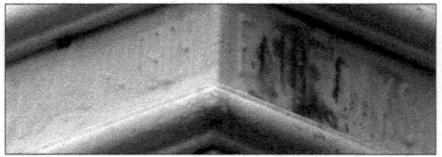

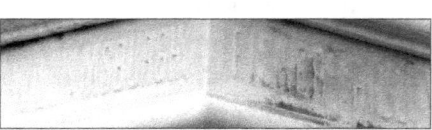

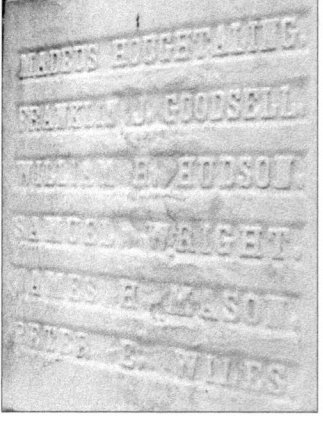

Worcester Monument

SURRENDER AND AFTERMATH

Excerpt from a Letter from John S. Kidder of Laurens to his wife, Harriet Kidder (in Subdued by the Sword by James M. Greiner)
March 30, 1865

Camp of the 121st Regt. N. Y.
9 P. M.

Dear Wife,

I have a few words to write as we have rec'd orders this hour from Lt. Col. Olcott that we shall have to storm the enemies works tomorrow morning by daylight. We shall probably move out of our camp about midnight. I think from the plan of battle we shall not have the worst place in the line. I shall leave this letter in the hands of our Quartermaster who will, if I fall, forward it to you. I hope to survive the contest but God only knows. I feel in good spirits. If I should fall do not mourn for me. I leave you and my little girls in much better circumstances than many fathers do. I feel that it is not any more for me to die for my country than it was for poor Brother George or thousands of others. I do not know of anything more to write. Kiss my little Girls for me and bring them up, educate them well. I hope to come home and see them.

Yours truly,
J. S. Kidder

Excerpt from the Journal of Seth Flint of Worcester
April 9th, 1865

A currior came riding through the smoke of battle carrying a white flag with a dispatch from Gen. Lee to Gen. Grant requesting an interview. We met him at Appomattox between the two lines of Blue and Gray as every gun was silenced and the smoke of battle began to clear away.

It happened that I was the only bugler present, and so I went along, much to my satisfaction, for I was eager to see the great leader of the Southern cause. [Lieutenant Colonel Orville E.] Babcock, carrying a white flag, such as it was, took his place beside [Captain] Mason and me, and off we went toward the enemy lines. I carried my bugle in one hand to sound the call to arms if we found that the Johnnies were trying to escape. That call would have been echoed all along our lines, and it would have been suicidal for them if they attempted a getaway, for the Federal troops had them bottled up and outnumbered five to one.

When I sounded taps, that sweetest of bugle calls, the notes had scarely died away when from the distance - it must have been from General Lee's headquarters - came, silvery clear, the same call; and, despite the sadness of the hour to the boys on the other side, I have a notion that they, like the Yanks, welcomed the end of hostilities and the coming of peace.

Letter from Amasa Cook Myrick of Gilbertsville to his Father April 13, 1865

City Point Va.

Dear Father

Doubtless you are somewhat surprised at not hearing from me before this. The truth is we have been on a very grand move and have scarcely had time to write and if I wished to ever so much I could not for the want of materials to do it with.

We broke camp on Wednesday March 9th and commenced moving towards the left of our line until we arrived at Hatcher Run where we commenced moving by the flank to the front It commenced to rain at night and for two days we were wet to the skin we continually drive the Enemy but encountered no works to any amount and did not loose many men. At this time the 5th Corps and Sheridans Command were on our left flank there was some skirmishing all the time but we kept them on the drive nothing of importance transpired of much account until the morning of the 2nd of April when we entered the works of the enemy where they had been driven and flanked out the same day we captured the connecter South Side R.R. such cheering as sent the air enemy once felt first rate we were then almost sure of the fate of Lee's arm the next day Petersburg was evacuated the next Richmond fell It would have done the north good to see the brave boys tired hungry cheering lustily

We marched very hard all the time but every one was in good spirits nothing now remained for us but to sever Lee's communications on the Danville R. R. at Burkesville Junction which was done and we knew that Lee must surrender for he had no way to feed his men and on Sunday April 9th Lee Surrendered his whole force and everything in & belonging to his command. They were paroled on the spot at Appomattox Court House and were allowed to return to their homes never again to take up arms against the U. S. until properly exchanged all officers were allowed to retain their side arms and personal property and baggage on Wednesday the 5th had to leave the Regiment and get in the Ambulance being literally played out my feet were very sore I kept in rear of the column until last Sunday when I was sent to Burkesville with the rest to be sent to this place we had to wait there for two days until the tracks could be altered from Petersburg we had the honor of being on the first train down Preceded by Genl Grant & staff

Our Regiment lost heavily in out fight what will be the disposition of the army when this is known I shall return to the Regt I am almost as well as ever but I must close write soon and accept this from your son

Direct as before
To the Regt
Lieut A Cook Myrick

Excerpt from the Diary of Lansing B. Paine of New Lisbon

April 19th, 1865 Wed.

Started from Annapolis, Md. About five o'clock in the morning attend the funeral of President Lincoln. Was very huge. Delegations from Pennsylvania, New York, & many other states present. The Army & Navy were well represented. We came back to Annapolis at night.

Letter from Cyrus J. Hardaway of Pittsfield to his Mother
May 21, 1865

Washington D. C.

Dear Mother

I received your letter & a little lecture on Thursday. I was glad I got it for I had felt the need of one for a long time. I think it has done me good for I feel a great deal better than I did before. I suppose that you have heard that there is to be a grand review in the City on Tuesday & Wednesday. I really wish that you could be here to see it for it will be a grand Sight. There will probably be more troops together here than there ever will be again in this Country. We shall probably be mustered out of the service in course of a month. I have not seen Foote since last Sunday. I guess he is all right. I shall go over & see him this afternoon. Col Per Lee & his wife got back from Utica yesterday. I think she must like soldiering pretty well. We are having plenty of ladies society now. Tow or three of the officers have got their wives down here & there are two very pleasant families close to camp so that we get an invitation out nearly Every Evening. Strawberries & Cherries are getting very plenty and quite cheap. I would like to send you a nice basket of them but I could without their being spoiled. I suppose when I began to write that I was going to make out a good long letter but my ideas have all vanished & I can not make out more than half a letter this time. I am very glad to hear that Libbie is getting along so well. Tell Summers that I would like to hear from him. I will answer all the letters that he will write. Have you heard anything from Peleg yet. Please let me know how he is getting along. Please remember me to all the family

Your Affectionate Son
CJ Hardaway

Letter from
James Connoford of Butternuts to Amasa Cook Myrick
May 25, 1865

Saratoga

Dear Friend Cook

Your very kind letter of March was received in due season I was very happy to learn that your health was good at that time and now rejoice to know that the war is about finished up and you are still a sound man.

I would have written on the receipt of your letter but I expected every week to be my last in Butternuts and hoped I would see you with the regiment. I ran round so much while in Butternuts that I could not tell you where to direct a letter. My health is now good, except that my limbs are inclined to swell considerable and my joints get so weak and stiff after a little exercise that I am at times troubled to navigate. Your father is well. All the boys are well

How do you feel after the review. Do you think the regiment will be discharged before a great while

I am told it is the intention of the U. S. Government to disband the army of the Potomac about the first of June I will if I can possible go to Washington in about three weeks I know not whether they will give me my discharge or not. I got my furlow extended twice but now intend to report back to Annapolis as soon as my leave expires. I have now to ask a request of you, that you will ask Michael Fitzgerald for $14 which he owes me, and ask John Flanagan for $12.00 I am in need of a little money as I have not received any pay in 15 months

When poor Fred Howard was about to die he left a paper requesting me to collect some money that was due to him in the Company & Regiment

Will you be so kind as to ask Wm. K. Helmer for $20 which he owed Fred and D. Groesbeck $6.80 should the regiment be disbanded it would be hard work to collect it, so do what you can and I will make it all right with you.

Edward Brooks $5.50 – Col Whistler $8.89 Doctor How $7.15 there is about $60 in small sums which it would be impossible to get. Do what you can to get the above.

The regiment fund was in to Fred $20 and Company fund $7.00

I have no news, write soon as you can & oblige

Your friend,
James Connoford
Saratoga Springs N. Y.
Care Messrs Brooks & Halbert

Cook do all you can to get that money from Helmer, Brooks and D. Groesbeck

Excerpt from *The Third Annual Report of the Bureau of Military Statistics of the State of New York* February 3, 1866

As Cherry Valley is the oldest town in Otsego county, and distinguished for her suffering in the Revolution, so she was the first to respond to the call for 75,000 men after the fall of Sumter. She raised a company and tendered its services, but it was not accepted owing to the organizations of what was known at Albany as skeleton regiments. The company, after being in barracks for some time, were disbanded, and several of the men enlisted in other organizations. Two of the young men active in raising this company, Olcott and Campbell, and who were the lieutenants, subsequently enlisted as privates in the Forty-fourth (Ellsworth) and by successive promotions became Colonels - the former of the famous One hundred and twenty-first New York, and the latter of the twenty-third United States Colored troops, and a member of the Army Board at Washington. In the course of the summer of 1861, large numbers of young men enlisted both in the infantry and cavalry-especially in the Mix (3rd) and Ira Harris (5th) cavalry. Eight or ten young men, representing some of the principal families in Cherry Valley and Cooperstown, enlisted as privates in the Forty-fourth. With one or two exceptions, all rose to be field or line officers and all thus promoted, were either killed, wounded or prisoners in Southern prisons. The bodies of more than half of them were brought back for sepulture in their native valleys. In the fall and winter of 1861-62, there was a recruiting station in Cherry Valley and three companies were raised for the Seventy-sixth New York - one company, of Berdan's sharpshooters was also organized at Cherry Valley, and most of the men enlisted in that vicinity. The First and Second Lieutenants, both afterwards captured, and brothers, were killed in battle and their remains lie in the Cherry Valley burying ground. Up to the time of the establishment of the senatorial or military districts, Otsego County had furnished about one thousand men. In 1862 Otsego and Herkimer raised the One hundred and twenty-first and One hundred and fifty-second, the former under the command of Colonel now Major-General Upton, was known in the army of the Potomac as Upton's regulars, and was a regiment greatly distinguished in that grand army. It proved its gallantry and left its blood in profusion on almost every battle-field. Of the One hundred and twenty-first and One hundred and fifty-second, Otsego furnished nearly fifteen hundred men. Before, the first draft she had sent about 2500 men to the field, almost all of them native-born sons of the county. This was a large contribution from an agricultural county, with no cities and no floating population. She responded to all the orders for drafts.

Excerpt from "War Reminiscences" by Delevan Bates (published in *The Otsego Republican*, October 25, 1895)

They (the members of the 152d N. Y. Volunteers) lost but few prisoners; the death roll is what decimated their ranks. This is the reason why the 152d, although a good regiment, never could be classed with the three hundred fighting regiments. The number killed on the battlefield did not reach the standard required. One hundred and thirty killed was the least number that the regiments called the "fighting regiments" counted when the war was ended, while the greatest loss was two hundred and ninety-five. The 121st could count two hundred and twenty six on this list, while the 152d only numbered sixty-nine. More were taken prisoners in the 152d than in the 121st, and perhaps more recovered from their wounds.

Excerpt from *The West Winfield Gazette*, March 6, 1914

The Nineteen Soldiers of Plainfield

A week ago the news came to Winfield of a good man gone, and he a soldier of the civil war - William Henry Nye, of the Wharton Valley. There were nineteen young men and boys who went from the town of Plainfield, as soldiers in the 121st New York Infantry. Now that Nye is gone, T. J. Hassett and the writer of these lines are the only survivors of the nineteen. Those people who are nearing the 70 mark, will remember those stirring times of the civil war when the young men went out by the hundreds to fight for the honor of the "Old Flag", and they saw to it that not a star was struck from its folds. The 121st N. Y. was raised in the counties of Otsego and Herkimer in the summer of 1862, and on the 30th of August this regiment, a thousand strong, left Herkimer for the _____ of war along the Potomac and Rapahannock rivers. On the 14th of Sept. these men were at the battle of South Mountain, Md., and three days later at Antietam. In December following, the 121st was at Fredericksburg, where Edward R. Spicer of Plainfield and Asahal Davis of Winfield were killed. In a word, the 121st became one of the fighting regiments of the war, losing 226 men killed during its term of service. Perhaps it would be well to give a brief account of the Plainfield men who were of that famous regiment.

Of the nineteen, nine were struck by Rebel bullets.

Of the nine, four were killed in battle.

Of the nineteen, ten were spared to return to their homes at the close of the war.

Andrew J. Hubbard - Mortally wounded at Salem Church, Va., May 3d, 1863. In this engagement the 121st lost ninety-seven men killed.

Chas. H. Tarbell - Went from Unadilla Forks. For many years after his return from the war he was with the firm of Chas. H. Childs & Co. of Utica.

B. F. Matteson - Went from Plainfield Center. Married, had a wife and three children. One of those children is now David Matteson of Brookfield.

John Curley - Brother of Martin Curley of Exeter. Accidentally drowned at Baltimore, Md.

Edward R. Spicer - Killed at Fredericksburg, Dec. 12, 1862. He was the first man of the 121st to fall before the enemy's fire.

Oscar A. Spicer - Brother of Edward R., died of diptheria at Hagerstown, Md., on the same day that Edward R. was killed.

John H. Reynolds - Wounded at the Wilderness, May 6, 1864. He went from his home at Port Chester, N. Y., to Gettysburg, to attend the 50th Anniversary of the battle. Arrived there June 29th last, and died of heart trouble on the evening of that day.

Dorr J. Devendorf - Was seventeen years old when he enlisted. He was a rugged lad and made one of the best soldiers of the regiment. He was killed at Spottsylvania, May 10th, 1864. For nearly fifty years he has been sleeping with the unknown dead.

William Kelty - When a boy he lived under the brow of Mt. Markham. He was always ready for duty, whether marching or fighting. He was one of the ninety-seven men killed at Salem Church.

Chas. C. Peet - Was well known in Plainfield before and after the war. He was wounded at Salem Church and came near losing an arm. Charley Peet and wife died years ago, their only child a daughter, Mrs. Elizabeth Swift, lives in Oklahoma.

Thomas Williams - Brother of John Williams (the Hill) lived on the Columbus Morgan farm near Spauldings. He contracted lung trouble while in service and did not live many years after the war.

John Hughes - Was a neighbor of Tom Wlliams. As soldiers they were like two brothers, tenting together and touching elbows through three years of service. John Hughes had hardly seen a sick day as a soldier, but he was taken ill about the time he received his discharge after Lee's surrender. He started for home when he should have been in a hospital. He reached Utica but could go no further. He died with friends in that city, but was denied the privilege of reaching that home of which he had dreamed for three long years. John Hughes was the brother of Mrs. Lewis Charles and Mrs. Hugh Owens of West Winfield.

William Hassett - A young man of good caliber, who was of the color guard of his regiment. At Salem Church when the Color Sargeant was shot down, Wm. Hassett took the flag and carried it until he too was wounded. After the war he became one of the best citizens and business men of the state of Missouri.

Thomas J. Hassett - Younger brother of Wm. At Upton's charge at Spottsylvania, he was wounded and carried from the field. For meritorious conduct on the field of battle, he was promoted to Captain. He was with his regiment when Lee surrendered at Appamattox.

William Henry Nye - Lived in the Wharton Valley all the years of his long life, save that period when he was a soldier. He was the 7th man of the nineteen to receive his final muster-out. Not many days ago he was laid to rest beside his father in that quiet city of the dead, the Huntley cemetery - a cemetery that he passed and repassed so many times as a boy and man. Peace to his ashes.

Alonzo Coon - There were eight of the nineteen who were boys of 18 years of less. Lonny Coon was one of the eight. He lived at Unadilla Forks, where he had never been from home a night until he went as a soldier. He died of that malady that doctors remedies will not heal, homesickness, for it is an ailment of the heart and mind and not of body. If he could have gone back to his mother's home for a week and slept in the little bed under the roof where the patter of rain had lulled him to sleep so many times, he would have been himself again. But the doctors of the regiment had no sympathy for him - they would not even send him to a hospital, and so he died - died of sheer homesickness.

James B. Warren - Lived in the Huntley neighborhood near the Frank Johnson cheese factory. He died of an attack of measles while in winter quarters at White Oak Church, Va.

Jacob Kehrer - A quiet German boy who tried to do his duty well. He died at the Soldiers Home at Bath, N. Y., in August last.

Dennis A. Dewey - Was known as one of the Dewey boys of Plainfield Center, when the civil war came to us. He was in every engagement of the 121st up to the Wilderness in May, 1864, where he was wounded and taken prisoner. Four days after the battle the Rebls chopped off his good right leg and kept him a prisoner for five months - three months of the time at Lynchburg, Va. Later on he was an unwilling guest at the "Hotel Libby," Richmond. He was paroled and sent into God's country in time to cast his first ballot for the reelection of Abraham Lincoln, in Nov., 1864. He is duly thankful and humbly grateful to have been spared these many years to write these lines today.

Excerpt from *The Daily Star*, October 26, 1932

William H. Colegrove, Last G. A. R. Post Member, Dies In Otsego Co. at Age of 88

Laurens – The last member of Brown Post, G. A. R., passed on to join his former comrades-in-arms on Wednesday, when William H. Colegrove, 88, died at the home of his grandson, Charles Trask , in Maryland, Otsego County.

He was born in Masonville on Feb. 1, 1844, a son of Phineas and Eliza Jane Palmer. In 1863, a youth of 18, he managed to enlist at Elmira in Company F of the 13th New York Regiment. He was transferred to Company K of the New York Heavy Artillary and served with that unit throughout the remainder of the war. His regiment, under Capt. George W. Ingalls, took part in several major engagements. Returning home after the way, He joined Brown Post of the G. A. R., organized at Schenevus.

Burial was in Maryland Cemetery, where the military services at the grave were under the auspices of Company G. 10th Infantry, New York National Guard.

Written for the Seventeenth Annual Reunion of Company E, 2nd N. Y., Heavy Artillery

Comrades we are to-night
To talk over old times once more,
For eight and twenty years have passed
Since the closing of the war.

We were young those days, and full of grit
When the south began to fuss,
No thought of danger or of death
In those times troubled us.

For love of country we left our homes
And marched onward for the front,
There in the thickest of the fight
Our enemies did confront.

In battles lost and battles won,
The land with blood made rich,
We fought the rebs until we drove
Them into their last ditch.

And then came Appomattox,
All hopes of victory past,
General Lee he did surrender
To General Grant at last.

The Union saved, one flag for all
Waving o'er the brave and free,
There came with the troops a marching home
The remnant of Company E.

A few names I'll mention from their roll,
Then you can hear and see
What a bully lot of boys they had
In the ranks of Company E.

Our comrade, Charles A. Hurlbutt,
Joined the silent majority,
One of the bravest of the boys
Who fought with Company E.

He stood by the guns, was captured,
Inside of Libby he did see,
Paroled, exchanged, again he joined
His comrades of Company E.

Then Lucius T. Bushnell.
Promoted for Bravery,
Was commissioned first lieutenant,
And assigned to Company E.

L. M. Bryant when taken prisoner,
Of Andersonville had a sight,
They tried to starve him, but they failed,
For he is here with us to-night.

And here is Theodore Musson,
A young soldier boy was he,
But bound to fight for the old flag
He too joined Company E.

N. S. Donaldson filled the bill
In every situation,
Always on hand at any time
To fall for his ration.

O. Briggs, a good boy in camp or out,
Well liked by all was he,
So full of fun the boys called him
The crack joker of Company E.

There are many more that I could name,
But it might weary you,
One could fill volumes with deeds
There were done by the boys in blue.

And then how honest these boys were
When they went from camp a walking,
Was never caught any tricks.
That's right, the truth I'm talking.

No smoke house raiding after hams,
And all chickens they let be,
No squealing heard from any hog,
So honest, honest was Company E.

A sample these Columbia's sons
Who fought on land and sea,
Thousands of men in the service then
Just like old Company E.

> Brave boys they saved the Union,
> And our glorious banner too,
> Let all arise and give three cheers
> For the boys who wore the blue.
>
> Company E, the time's approaching
> When we'll march for the other shore,
> If our record's clean our re-union there
> Will last for evermore.
>
> Yours in F. C. and L., V. P.

Remarks of Robert Consigli, President of the Abner Doubleday Civil War Roundtable, Re-dedication of the Cherry Valley Civil War Monument May 28, 2011

The people of Cherry Valley knew that when the Civil War ended in 1865 that the United States was forever changed and the soldiers who had volunteered made that change possible. The Monument was dedicated in 1868 and lists the men of Cherry Valley who served in the units from that area. These units were the 76th, 121st, 152nd Volunteer Infantries and the 3rd United States Cavalry. The monument also lists those battles where these units served, such as Gettysburg, Wilderness, Petersburg and Appomattox. Over 2,000 men from Otsego County answered the call to serve their country.

General Grant, in his farewell message to Union soldiers, issued on June 2, 1865, anticipated how the nation would remember the war.

"Soldiers of the Armies of the United States! By your patriotic devotion to your country in the hour of danger and alarm—your magnificent fighting, bravery, and endurance—you have maintained the supremacy of the Union and the Constitution, overthrown all armed opposition to the enforcement of the Law, and of the Proclamations forever Abolishing slavery, the cause and pretext of the Rebellion, and opened the way to the Rightful Authorities to restore Order and inaugurate Peace on a permanent and enduring basis on every foot of American soil."

Grant also recognized the sacrifices that these men made and expressed how the nation would remember their devotion to the cause. He expressed his desire that the nation cherish and support their stricken families. Although the monument stands today with faded names and events, we in re-dedicating this monument, should never forget what they achieved—preservation of the Union and freedom for all people.

Above: Robert Consigli lays a wreath during the ceremony. Opposite page: Civil War re-enactors at the ceremony. Photos of the monument appear on the following page.

Cherry Valley Monument

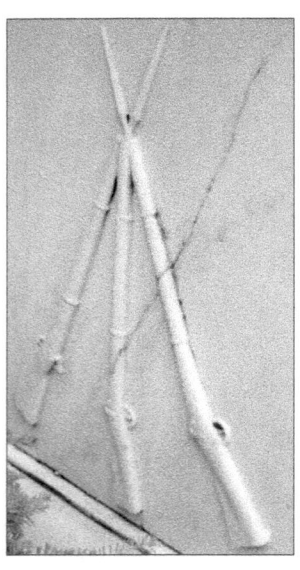

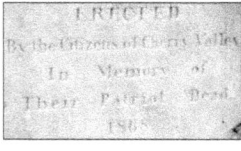

APPENDIX I: MEN FROM OTSEGO COUNTY SELECTED FOR THE DRAFT

Men selected from Otsego County for the draft during the Civil War from the Oneonta Herald, September 9-23, 1863, organized by town.

Burlington

168 names in wheel, 50 drawn. 1st Artillery, Co. A; 2nd Artillery, Co. L; 121st Infantry, Co. K.; 152nd Infantry, Co. I.

H. E. Aylesworth	Jacob Goey	John D. Pierson
Warren Babbitt	James H. Hall	William L. Prentiss
David Benjamin	William Hall	Russel Rexford
Seth H. Benjamin	Frastus Hanor	Reuben Rogers
Daniel L. Bolton	Wesley Herrington	Aaron M. Rood
Noah D. Bolton	A. M. Holdredge	John Shinker
William Breese	Aaron D. Hubbell	Albert Shipenan
Philip Brown	Solomon Huestis	James Smart
Charles Burdick	Robert F. Hume	William Spicer
Lorenzo Burick	Charles M. Johnson	Duane Sprague
Benjamin Cahoon	Nathan Joslyn	James M. Sprague
William Clark	Thomas Lough	Albert Talbot
Lorenzo Clock	Albert Main	Daniel M. Talbot
Robert Cockburn	Newton A. Marcy	Ed Van Steenberg
Alonzo J. Darby	Peter McRory	Robert G. Wallace
Fayete Fitch	James H. Meacham	Dwight Webater

Butternuts

176 names in wheel, 52 were drawn. 121st Infantry, Co. K; 152nd Infantry, Co. G; 179th Infantry, Co. C.

David Adams	Calvin T. Eastman	Horatio Littlefair
Orson Adams	Leander Emerson	T. A. Lockwood
Charles H. Allen	Le Grand Emmons	Win K. Mead
Andrew G. Backman	Edward Gadsby	John C. Morris
William Bard	James T. Gadsby	Edwin Morso
Abel O. Barnes	John H. Gadsby	Daniel Niles
Francklin Beardsley	John Garlick	Enos Peabody
Samuel Birdsal	Alonzo L. Hakes	J. Raymond
James R. Blackman	Asel A. Halbert	Henry Rodman
Henry O. Braver	Henry R. Halbert	Charles P. Root
Simeon Church, Jr.	Bradley N. Hanford	John P. Sawyer
Harmon Coon	Osborne Harris	Ransford Sharts
Thomas K. Cope	Robert Haynes	Henry Slade
Albert Cornell	Gould Hurlbut	David O. Starr
Jared C. Cox	Henry R. Hurlbut	John Stebbins
Lucius Coye	Philip Jackson	James Turner
Samuel R. Curr	Charles Jay	
Henry D. Donaldson	John J. Kinne	

Cherry Valley

277 names in wheel, 80 drawn. 121st Infantry, Co. E & G; 3rd Artillery, Co. M; 6th Cavalry, Co. D & E.

Isaac A. Allan	George Cloxton	Edwin P. Gardner
Daniel Alter	John Colver	Smith Gordon
Thomas Ashton Jr.	Jeremiah Crettenden	John Hardendorf
Phillip J. Ball	Robert Davidson	George Head
Henry Banker	Philip Diefendorf	Delevan E. Hills
Wing V. S. Bastian	William Drain	Peter D. House
Lyman W. Bates	Eben Eggleston	John F. Hubbard
Tobias Baxter	Menzo Elliott	Joseph O. Hubbard
C. Bellman	Albert Flint	Dennis Kilfoil
James Boyce	Joseph Flint	Thomas Lake
William K. Brown	Nelson Flint	Stephan H. Lettis
William Burch	Peter Folnn	James O. Lewis
James S. Campbell	Jacob Fox	John J. Lumley
Thomas Clark	Peter Fox	Thomas Lynk
John Cling	James Galt	Lorin Marks

Appendix I: List of Men Drafted from Otsego County

Dennis McCarthey	Thomas Rowe	Fred Ullman Jr.
John H. McKillopp	Norman Rutt	Aaron Van Dyck
Albert McPhee	Albert Shaul	George Walby
Ezra McPhee	Russel Sherman	Levi Waldrat
William H. McPhee	Thomas S. Shields	George W. Wendell
Jackson Millson	John H. Smith	J. A. Whillis
John W. Mitchell	Josiah Snyder	Theron Wickham
Andrew J. Moore	John Spencer	Daniel C. Wilson
Henry Moore	Olivier C. Spencer	Alonzo Woodward
George Pegg	James Spraker	Adam Yager
John Pegg	Peter Stewart	
Wellington Riley	Benjamin Ullman	

Decatur

77 names in wheel, 20 drawn. 121st Infantry, Co. G.

Henry W. Boorne	George Fern	James Rury
Lorenzo Chapin	John R. Flint	Jorace Scutt
James Daley	Riley T. Flint	William Simmons II
Alonzo Dana	Justus Lewis	Robert S. Skinner
Jay Davenpeck	Horace B. Lum	A. Van Voorhees
Asa Day	Jonathan P. Montgomery	John D. White
George Devenpeck	Alex Rury	

Edmeston

173 names in wheel, 52 drawn. 1st Artillery, Co. A; 121st Infantry, Co. F.

William Adams II	Noyes Dye	Joseph H. Page
J. H. Allenderf	Spencer R. Dye	Edward L. Peck
Charles W. Allendorf	Nathaniel W. Gallop	William S. Peck
Charles Bass II	N. L. Green	George M. Pitta
Eoster H. Bilyea	Albert J. Hills	Charles H. Pope
Amenzo R. Brown	Samuel Hoxie	Alonzo Preston II
Emmit Chapin	Solomon Hoxie II	Chester Reynolds
Peter Chapin	Edward Jordon	Jared Robinson
William Chase	Andrew Kelsey	Edward J. Shermerhorn
Amos Colgrove	James L. Manchester	Henry Sheldon
Warren Colgrove	Truman L. Matterson	Alburtus Simmons
Elisha B. Crandall	Normal Mitchell	James M. Simmons

Marshall Simmons
Oramel Spaffard
Hiram Spicer
James B. Spurr
Eric Talbot
George W. Talbot

Richmond Talbot
Truman Taylor
Charles Weaver
Charles Welch
Dennison P. Welch
John Wheeler

John White
George H. Whitmore
Leander Wight
Charles Williams

Exeter

141 names in wheel, 41 drawn. 2nd Artillery, Co. L; 121st Infantry, Co. F; 152nd Infanttry, Co. G.

Edward Andrews
John Andrews
Irwin J. Angell
Henry H. Beadle
William H. Bristol
Orlando D. Brooks
Alonzo Brown
Thomas G. Burgess
Taber Card
Floyd C. Childs
Byron Cole
Lorenzo Colt
Webber J. Colt
Fred G. Crecey

George R. Cushman
Orlando D. Davenport
John Duel
Cortes S. Gates
Orin Haight
William B. Hal
Malcolm Higby
George W. Hines
Osmar W. Hines
Truman H. Hines
Marcus D. Johnson
Burton W. Lidell
Charles H. Newkirk
David Newkirk

S. Newman
George Porter
Abraham J. Roof
George D. Rose
Melvern Rose
William Rose
John J. Ryder
Marcus S. Southworth
Lee C. Stone
Ira Sutherland
Elis Town
Henry M. Watkins
Auger Williams

Hartwick

211 names in wheel, 65 drawn. 3rd Artillery, Co. M; 121st Infantry, Co. E & I; 152 Infantry, Co. H & I.

Jerome Atwell
Amos Barton
Delos Beckley
Henry Billderbeck
Edwin A. Bissell
Thomas Bonner
Edwin Bowe
George Brownell II
James Camp
Benjamin Carr
Chester Carr

Theodore Carr
Edwin Collar
John L. Converse
Robert Davison
Francis Drew
Rensselaer Duncar
John Dunlap
Thomas Edmonds
John Eldrid
Albert Evans
Henry C. Field

Orsen Field
Benjamin Fisk
Robert Gardner
Omey Gifford
John Goodrich
Thomas Gowey
Merton Green
Hiram House
Hollis Howe
Norton Jacobs
John W. Lake

John Lippitt
James Leonard
George Luther
Marens Luther
Melville Marles
Henry Miller
George W. Murdock
Hiram Murdock
Morgan S. Northrop
Benjamin Owens
Mark A. Perry
Willard Pickens
Ashel H. Potter
David J. Putnam
Patrick Riley
Zobediah Salisbury
William H. Shove
Sidney Smith
William H. Smith
Robert Telfer
Edwin Todd
James E. Todd
Horace Van Styke
Abraham Vorhees
Jason T. Wallace
Henry Ward
Samuel Ward
Adelbert Wells
Amos Wells
G. W. Wentworth
David P. Wicks
Lewis Wood

Laurens

208 names in wheel, 58 drawn. 121st Infantry, Co. I & K; 152nd Infantry, Co. H & I.

Henry Ackley
Thomas Alver
Peterson Barton Jr.
Richard Benson
Emmons Bridges
Erastux Brightman
Morris Butts
George W. Card
Zepham Cogahell
William Comstock Jr.
Robert Cook
Richard J. Cooley
Melville Coye
Orlo Coye
Philip Decker
Lester Easton
John Eckerson
Lytham Eldred
Solomon Eldred
Elisha Fisher
John R. Fisk
Albert Field
Delos Fryon
Charles Fuller
Charles Gardner
Nathaniel Gardner
Edwin Gulle
Abel Harrington
Delon Harrington
Guy H. Haskins
Willard Hathaway
Horace Hill
Richard Hoke
David Johnson
Charles Kenyon
Harlow Lyon
Charles Merrill
Vincent Miller
Charles Myers
George Naylor
Richard Nearing
Ensign Nichols
John Phelps
James Priest
Tabor Richardson
Truman Root
Ezra Rowland
Zebulon Sarton
Erastas St. John
E. Schermerhorn
Emery L. Smith
Eldridge Stanton
Charles Sylvester
Eugene Thayer
Chauncey Tucker
George Van Buren
Daniel Westherbee
George Woolhonse

Maryland

209 names in wheel, 61 drawn. 121st Infantry, Co. I & K; 152nd Infantry, Co. H & I.

Fred J. Aldrich	Lewis Grassfield	George R. Shears
Judson Bains	Chester Gurney	George Shutts
Levi Boardman	Hiram Gurney	Edgar Smallin
Delevan Bonnett	Abraham Halbut	John B. Smith
Riley Bostwick	Levi L. Hazen	Alex Somerville
David M. Brando	William Hazen	Rob Somerville
John Buchanan	William H. Holdridge	Israel Spencer
Lester Burnside	Benjamin Hoos	Phillip B. Spencer
William W. Burnside	Orrin Johnson	Alex Strain
Edwin Cass	Orrin Lamphire	Calvin Thorp
Henry Chambelain	John Lee	George Tubbs
Milton Chambelain	Banner J. Marble	Charles Utter
Azro Chase	Hannibal K. Morse	John Wade
Erastus G. Chase	Dennis Noonan	Judson Walling
R. C. Chase	Fred E. Palmer	Henry Wany
Ariel Clark	John Peebles	Owen B. Webster
Ephriam Dunham	Lambert Rathbon	William R. Whiting
George W. Dunham	Levi G. Rockway	Elias Wickham
Alonzo B. Every	Nathan Rockway	George Witt
Franklin M. Fox	James Rose	
Sylvester Gornish	Thomas Russell	

Middlefield

343 names in wheel, 103 drawn. 22nd Cavalry, Co. L; 121st Infantry, Co. E. & G; 2nd Mounted Rifles, Co. M.

Arthur Antisdale	Albert Burton	William Colling II
Edwin M. Bailey	Samuel Burton	George Cooper
Adelbert C. Barnum	Benjamin Butler	Judson W. Cornish
Charles C. Barnum	Jerome Butler	George Crandall
E. D. Barnum	Lot Camp II	Thomas Crandall
Dorr M. Bates	Henry Campbell	James Delancey
John J. Belknapp	Jonas J. Campbell	Alvin Eckler
Simon Bennett	William Case	Jay Eckler
David Bice	John O. Cass	William Eggleston
Albert Boyce	William P. Clark	George Filkins
Lyman Buel	LeRoy Clide	Hiram Fitz

Appendix I: List of Men Drafted from Otsego County

John Fitz
John Gardner
Emerson Gaylor
Jos. Goodenough
John M. Graham
Clement Guy
George Guy II
Harry Guy
Richard Hand
William Hannas
Richard Holcomb
Morris Holdredge
James Holliday
Fernando Hubbell
G. A. Hubbell
Melville G. Hubbell
Delroy A. Hunter
Richard Hutchins
Selon E. Isman
Henry Jones
George Leal
John Leonard
George Ludlum
George Mallory
James W. Manktlow
Delos Manzer
Collins S. Marks
Norman L. Mason
James McDonald II
Elias McKnown
Philander Moak
Samuel Morrison
John S. Newton
James G. North
George Ostrander
George G. Palmer
Renselaer Palmer
Adriel Parshall
Albert Parshall
Levi Parshall
Henry Pay
Charles B. Reed
Daniel E. Reynolds
John Reynolds
George Risendorf
Frederic Rogers
Lewis Rowland
William Ryan
J. W. Saxton
Delbert Sherman
Clark Smith
John D. W. Smith
John W. Smith
G. A. Springsteed
Daniel P. Temple
George Temple
E. Thomas (Col.)
James Van Bushkirk
William Van Bushkirk
Albert Vanderburg
Albert Van Deusen
C. M. Van Deusen
Peter V. Waldorf
William Webb
Lewis O. White
Amos Wickwire
William H. Winnie

Milford

255 names in wheel, 76 drawn. 3rd Artillery, Co. M; 121st Infantry, Co. E & I; 152nd Infantry, Co. H.

Augustus Ackley
Jerome Alger
Floyd Aylesworth
L. M. Aylesworth
Jerome E. Baker
Fred E. Barnard
Ellery H. Barney
John Barney
Elmer Bostwick
Gershom Bostwick
Andrew J. Bradley
Lorin T. Brown
John K. Burnett
F. H. Campbell
Marvin E. Clark
Lamber Coller
Jacob Collier
George Connolly
Nelson Cronkite
William Dixon
Warren Elliott
Lewis Ellis
Edmund R. Every
James Ferguson
Ray Green
Robert Hall
William C. Hanlon
Willis Houghtaling
Daniel House
A. L. Hubbard
Edwin Hubbard
Delos Hungerford
Hiram Hungerford
George Jackson
Henry Kenyon
Solomon Knapp
John McAuliff
James M. Mead
Leverett D. More
Ham H. Morgan
Albert Mumford
Wallace Mumford
William Munfonberg
Demon R. Packer
John Peaselee

Almon Peterson
George Potter
LeRoy H. Potter
M. Quackenbush
David Riffenberg
Lester Schermerhorn
Joseph M. Scott
Solomon Sergeant
Asa Silliman
Alonzo Sipperly

Conrad Sparker
Oscar Tallmadge
John J. Townsend
Peter H. Van Etten
Albro A. Waters
Edger Waters
Cortland Westcott
Emmet R. Westcott
Orlando Westcott
William White

William Wilcox
Walton A. Winser
Daniel Winsor
James Woodbeck
Walter Wright
Albert Yager
William Yager
Ben Yeomans
John S. Yeomans

Morris

105 names in wheel, 59 drawn. 121st Infantry, Co. I; 152nd Infantry, Co. G.

Sylvester D. Aldrich
Isaac Angell
Nathaniel B. Bagg
Stanley Bagg
Alva Bailey
Edwin Brooks
Luzerne Brooks
Walter Brooks
Cyrus E. Brown
Balias F. Burdick
Lyman Burr
Harrison Camp
George Churchill
Alvera Cook
John J. Cook
Tomas Cook
Porter Davis
Daniel H. Foot
George Foot
Milo Gross II

Erbert Harris
Henry W. Hendricks
Willard Holbrook
Eli Kinne
William K. Lippitt
Edward H. Lutt
Oliver J. Lutt
Levi McIntyre
Rufus Moddy
Fred B. Palmer
Samuel H. Poet
Gilbert Potter
Olney R. Potter
John Priest
Eugene S. Rergan
LeGrand Sanderon
Charles Sheff
Andrew J. Sholes
Anson Spafford
Silas S. Smith

Solomon Stephens
Murray S. Tallman
Charles T. Thorp
Adin Tilley
Josiah Tilson
Joseph E. Tobey
Stephen N. Toby
Henry Todd
Daniel Tracy
Eugene Tracy
Amos L. Turner
Gutman Weeden
Oscar Wightman
Charles F. Wilson
William A. Wilson
Stephan D. Wing
Jonish Withey
William Woodcock
George A. Yates

New Lisbon

137 names in wheel, 40 drawn. 121st Infantry, Co. K; 152 Infantry, Co. H & I; 176th Infantry, Co. G.

Mumford Aldrich	Adin Gregory	Richmond D. Potter
Isaac Alger	Isaac Gregory	James Priest
Amasa Balcom	Edgar Hinman	Dan C. Rockwell
John M. Bell	Henry D. Hinnian	Lander J. Rockwell
Damon A. Brown	Thomas Hall	Albert Smith
Elam Bundy	Aaron Harrington	Samuel Teht
Ziba Carlton	Thomas Hume	Sanford Thorp
George M. Chapin	David L. Johnson	William Telfor
Brayton Covey	John A. Knox	Jehiel J. Tilley
Richard T. Emerson	David W. Morse	Marion D. Tuller
Francis Follett	M. J. Morse	John G. Whipple
Morris Fowler	Orrin B. Nearing	Robert Young
Isaac N. Glendhill	Harvey Parkunt	
Lore J. Glendhill	Alberto Porter	

Oneonta

186 Names in wheel, 54 drawn. 43rd Infantry, Co. C; 121st Infantry, Co. K; 152nd Infantry, Co. G.

John Alger	Lester Emmons	A. J. Richardson
Harvey B. Arnold	Henry R. Gitford	William Richardson
Stephan Baker	Allen Green	Allen Scrambling
Dewitt Beams	Delos W. Green	Riley A. Sessions
John Beams Jr.	Leroy Hackett	Henry Shutters
Oscar Beach	Walter Hodge	John Sigsbee
L. A. Bissell	Isaac Holmes	George Snow
Andrew Bresee	T. Howard	Chauncey Staton
Martin Brownold	Lasell Jacobs	Elkanah Swart
Nathaniel Bull	J. McDongall	J. R. Thayer
Wesley W. Clark	Willard Morrell	Leroy Thayer
Abraham Couse	C. Munson	George Walker
Edge Couse	Nathaniel Niles	Henry Wilcox
Francis Crispel	O. H. Orr	G. A. Winne
Elvin Cutshaw	John T. Pardoe	Calvin Woodbeck
Orson Dean	Alonzo Pratt	Granville Yager
Charles Driggs	Jacob Quackenbush	Matthew Young
Lowellen Elliott	Gamaliel Reynolds	Stephan Young

Otego

159 names in wheel, 30 drawn. 90th Infantry, Co. E; 121st Infantry, Co. E. F. H. & K; 144th Infantry, Co. D; 152nd Infantry, Co. G.

Martin V. Briggs	S. J. Hess	Reuben S. Parish
John H. Brown	William L. Horton	Jacob Quackenbush
Ezra G. Brown	Theodore P. Horton	Albert Rockwell
John Case	Alfred Hough	Edward Root
George W. Cook	Wright Jay	Delos Scrambling
Charles Fleming	Carlton B. Lewis	Albert H. Sheldon
Samuel R. Follett	Calvin Livingston	Henry Trask
Harry Guy	Edward S. Murble	Justus Trask
Albert Harris	Stephen D. Northrop	Myron Wilcox
Alfred Hess	Edwin Parish	Charles S. Williams

Otsego

470 names in wheel, 136 drawn. 2nd Artillery, Co. L; 22nd Cavalry, Co. L; 3rd Infantry Co. C; 152 Infantry, Co. D, G, & I; 176th Infantry, Co. G.; 6th Cavalry, Co. G.

George Adam	C. Brockway	Horace Dunham
Alonzo Adams	William A. Brockway	Leverett Edmonds
Clark P. Adams	George Brooks	C. Ellsworth
Marius B. Angell	James Bunyar	Charles Fay
Joel W. Avery	Amos Campbell	Chester Fellows
William Bacon	Joseph Campbell	James P. Fern
Nelson Ballard	Josiah Case	Daniel Finch
Walter Bann	Thomas Chamberlin	Squire Keyes Jerome Fish
Alfred Barton	James Chappell	George H. Fitch
William H. B. Bassett (Col.)	Stephen Cheesebro	Albert Gardner
	Alanson P. Clark	Horace Getman
Albert H. Bates	Frank A. Clark (Col.)	William Gifford
Pulaski C. Bates	Eri S. Collar	Alonzo Hall
George Beadle	Miles E. Cook	Justin Hall
Levi Becker	William G. Cooley	Frank Hammond
Alfred Bliss	J. R. Coppernoll	Harvey Harrington
William Bliss	Elon Denis	Edward Higby
Dennis Bly	Ezra W. Dento	Alonzo House
Philander Bonesteel	Benjamin Dingman	Hiram House
Abraham Bowman	John A. Dingman	Joel House
Benjamin Brewer	Chauncey M. Drake	Menzo House

Appendix I: List of Men Drafted from Otsego County

Oscar Jones	Orville L. Plumb	Alson Taylor
Edward Joslyn	Rexford Potter	Morris Taylor
Irvin Kelley	John Potts	Thomas Taylor Jr.
John Lang	Milton Richards	Delos Thayer
George D. Lathrop	Thomas A. Ridley	William Thompson
Frederick G. Lee	Alfred E. Robbins	John H. Tice
Patrick Leonard	Truman Robinson	Norman Turner
W. Leonard	William Satterlee	Chester Tuttle
Don C. Lewis	Levi Secor	Chester I. Wadsworth
Michael Little	Lorenzo Seeber	James M. Walker
Morris McPhee	William Seeber	O. J. Walradt
Henry Merchant	William Shaul	Delos Warner
James Miller	Orrin Shawn	Edwin Webster
George Misson	Andrew Shepard	Martin Webster
Ransom Morfat	W. Sheppard	Charles Weldon
William J. Mursey	Barney Simmons	Judson Wheeler
John A. Myers	James Simmons	Thaddeus R. White
Jonathan Myers	Francis Smith	Harvey Williams
Delos Newkirk	Nelson Smith	Henry Williams (Col.)
George Newkirk	Lyman Spafard	Jonathan Williams (Col.)
Michael Owens	Ira T. Spencer	Joseph Winsor
Jolin M. Patten	John M. Stevens	Lewis Wood
George Peck	Armstrong Stinson	Ephraim Woodcock
Alexander Phillips	Delos Storing	John M. Young

Pittsfield

108 names in wheel, 31 drawn. 3rd Infantry, Co. C; 121st Infantry, Co. I & K; 152 Infantry, Co. H. Note: The Parish brothers were contraband (free blacks) and were specially invited.

Marcus Aylesworth	Sol W. Harrington	George H. Parish
Edwin M. Baird	Aaron J. Hong	Morris Parish
Hiram Barber	Leland Hurlbut	Prime Parish
William H. Church	Joe L. Kake	Jesse S. Patrick
George Elliott	Rufus Keller	Charles Richardson
James Ferguson	Joseph McLeish	Asshel B. Richaro
Joseph Ferguson	Thomas S. Miller	Henry W. Slocum
Thomas W. Fuller	Arthur Moore	Gruman Spafford
Edwin O. Green	Thomas H. Moore	Theodore Wilbar
William L. Green	Samuel M. Morse	
Zebulon Gregory	C. Murdock	

Plainfield

111 names in wheel, 31 drawn. 13th Artillery, Co. C; 121st Infantry, Co B & K; 146th Infantry, Co. G; 152nd Infantry, Co.

Charles H. Armstrong	Francis Crumb	William H. Nye
Delos C. Bass	Alfred Davis	Edwin B. Pearsoll
Andrew Briggs (Col.)	John C. Davis	William C. Richards
Andrew J. Brown	Irwin Dewey	Floyd W. Rogers
Murty Burns	John Donnelly	James Welch
Edwin L. Chapman	Daniel D. Dye	Hamilton J. Whitford
Edgar B. Clark	A. V. W. Fuller	Alfred M. Williams
Isaac P. Clark	George W. Giles	John Williams
Russell W. Clark	Evan James	Morris P. Williams
Stephen R. Clark	Peter Kinne	
James Colman	William Morris	

Richfield

174 names in wheel, 51 drawn. 2nd Artillery, Co. I; 16th artillery, Co. F; 121st Infantry, Co. H.

Nathan Ames	Norman Getman	Charles Palmer
O. H. P. Andrews	Timothy Greely	Eli Palmer
Chauncey Aple	Martin Griffin	Marion Perkins
W. T. Bailey	Eliad Hadseh	John Pottle
A. E. Barstow	D. W. Harrington	George W. Robinson
H. S. Bradly	E. D. Harrington	L. J. Robinson
Almon Brown	F. J. Harrington	William H. Rounds
Jerome Catlin	George Hatch	Elvaro Shaul
John Colwell	James Hoves	Damon Skinner
Thomas Croke	Jerome Hull	Horace Snydes
Peter Dash	Irvin Hunt	John Sternburgh
Charles Duffy	Alexander Hurdle	John Thatcher
John Dutilier	Thomas Hurky	Ephram Ward
L. T. Ely	William Johnson	Nicholas Weldon
M. C. Fontoc	A. B. Lee	Richard Weldon
James Foreman	Charles McReady	John Wright
Melvin Fuller	Kilburn Mumford	Addis Young

Roseboom

188 names in wheel, 56 drawn. 121st Infantry, Co. E & G; 152nd Infantry, Co. I & K

Asa Atkins
Ofa Bailey
Lewis Beach
Isaac Becker
William H. Beeger
John Bell
M. Alvarev Brown
William Burton
Harrison Butler
Seth Butler
Norman Chambers
Alfred Conrad
Joshua Conrad
J. Countryman
T. Dickerson
Ozias Eckerson
Zephaniah Eckerson
John A. Eldred
John G. Folen
Henry Fremyre
John Fremyre
James B. Gage
James B. Gaylor
Lewis M. Gillett
Harris Gillott
Jerome Granger
John Granmer
Hamilton Green
Myron Hall
William H. Hanson
George L. Howland
William H. Linacre
Harvey Lovejoy
Hiram Low
Othelbert Low
Arba Mabee
James Marsh
William S. Maston
Melvin M. Peeso
Edward Pierson
Adam Scrambling
William R. Seeber
Alex R. Sherman
Joseph Sisum
Joseph Sisum
Nicholas Snyder
Asa G. Spencer
Jacob G. Ullinan
J. W. Vandorwaker
Cort Van Schaick
John E. Ward
Andrew Winnie
Angevine Winnie
Delos Winnie
Mansfield Winnie
Redmond Wrin

Springfield

263 names in wheel, 77 drawn. 24th Cavalry, Co. B; 121st Infantry, Co. E; 152nd Infantry, Co. D, E & I

James Allen
Arthur B. Ayres
George T. Ayres
Douglas B. Branch
Calvin Brazee
Lucius Brink
David Brook
George W. Chappel
Squire Clark
Charles B. Coburn
Charles Conden
Farley Conety
Benoni R. Conklin
Josiah Cook
William Crosby
Patrick Cullen
Henry H. Dugleby
Monroe Dutcher
Theodore Elwood
Edward S. Francis
James Frost
Peter Gadeant
Marvin Gardnet
John Genter
Theodore L. Grant
Chester C. Grauger
John Graves
D. W. Gray
Lemuel B. Gray
Alexander Hadfock
Robert Harberson
William T. Hardy
Henry Heath
William Hoke
Cornelius S. Holmes
Charles S. Hood
Dexter Hood
John H. Host
Alonzo Hoyer
John J. Jackson
Lorenzo Kane
Newell Kelley

Charles Landon
Sanford Maxfield
Peter McCabe
John McIven
Alfred McRory
David McRory
Andrew Oliver
John Oliver
Peter S. Ostrander
David Phillips
Solomon Powers
Nicholas Riley
John Saxton
Charles Sawter
James W. Shipman
Herbert Small
Joseph H. Snyder
Martin Springer
Jesse Sullivan
Simon Tougheye
James Turner
Herman Van Auken
Martin Van Buren
John Walby
Anson Walter
Joel G. White
Geary Wightman
John Witsie
Joseph S. Whipple
Hiram R. Wood
Clement Wright
Garret Wyckoff
Grange H. Young
James H. Young
John Young

Unadilla

209 names in wheel, 69 drawn. 3rd Artillery, Co. L; 3rd Cavalry, Co. D; 10th Cavalry, Co. K; 22nd Cavalry, Co. L; 90th Infantry, Co. E; 121st Infantry, Co. F

Salas Alkins
Chester K. Allen
Anthony Alsop
Sylvester Arms Jr.
Franklin R. Arnold
Russell Aylesworth
Clinton G. Barnes
James Bartholomew
Josiah T. Beardsley
Lewis Bennett
James H. Birdsall
Reuben Brown
O. H. Buckley
Frank M. Burdick
Thomas Burdick
Franklin Bush
Lewis Carmichael
Benjamin Clapp
William H. Crane
George H. Crounse
John Delos Curtis
Charles Curtiss
Rinaldo Curtiss
Walter Curtiss
Lucias M. Davis
George W. Dibble
David Dunlap
Edwin J. Fancher
George B. Foot
T. S. Flint
Edward B. Gardner
Henry G. Gregory
Thomas Hallock
Henry W. Harris
Charles Hayes
Charles H. Haynes
Ezra Hemingway
Robert Hollis
Hobart Ives
William H. Juckett
John R. Kirkland
Frederick La Sure
Judson Lesure
Samuel Lewis
Joseph Linberger
James E. Meeker
James Neff
David Nickels
Marble Nichols
Lyman G. Osborn
George Ostrander
Benjamin Palmer
Joshua Palmer
Henry Parsons
James Raynor
Ira S. Sanders
David Sherwood
Rufus M. Sherwood
David Strong
John Van Deusen
David Van Schaick
George H. Sisson
George W. Thomas Jr.
Robert M. Van Schaick
Benjamin Webb
Stephen Wilbur
James T. Wilkins
Albert Young
Wheeler C. Youngs

Appendix I: List of Men Drafted from Otsego County

Westford

125 names in wheel, 35 drawn. 121st Infantry, Co. G.

Carlos Ashley	Horace C. Holmes	Eder Pierce
William Henry Badau	James C. Holmes	George N. Roberts
Moses D. Bently	Raselas Huskins	John K. Salsbury
Little Bostick	David Lee	Ira Sherman
Augustus Boyce	Thomas Maxwell	John R. Skinner
William Bradley	John C. Moak	Elisha C. Spafford
Alanson B. Campbell	John A. Nellis	Summer E. Tipple
Ira C. Carey	Mark Norton	Stephen Treat
Josiah G. Earl	Chris Palmier	George Tyes
David Fox	William Peak	Waldo H. Tyler
Rinaldo Green	Robert W. Peedles	Isaac Woodcock
David S. Herdman	Charles Pierce	

Worcester

192 names in wheel, 57 drawn. 121st Infantry, Co. G & I; 152nd Infantry, Co. I & K.

Elias Aikins	German A. Gott	Fordus Powers
John W. Albert	Seth H. Grant	Milton Powers
Oscar Alvoord	John H. Grote	Edger Prindle
Ansel Barney	John Hallenbake	Alexander Queal
Alexander Bates	Ezra Haynor	Edward Ridge
George Becker	A. H. Houghtaling	Francis Ridge
George H. Bellou	Hiram H. Hughes	John S. Ridge
Stephen A. Bernor	Leonard Jaycox	Ebenezer Sawyer
German C. Boorn	Schuyler Martin	John D. Shelland
James D. Boorn	Alex McClintock	Hezekiah Skinner
Barney Brazee	John McClintock	Edward Sloan
Elithu Burrill	William McClintock	Sylvester Smith
Marvin Buttle	Oliver J. Mowbray	William N. Smith
Ezra Cain	Henry Multer	William Spelman
Josiah Clark	Eti E. Nichols	James K. Strain
Edger Crippen	Wesley Nickel	Egbert Ten Eyck
Chelsea Davis	Erastus Pierce	Nelson Thurber
Cyrus Davis	Norman Pierce	Lyman Tiffany
Silas W. Dickinson	Thomas Platt	George White

APPENDIX II: MEDAL OF HONOR RECIPIENTS FROM OTSEGO COUNTY

Davidson, Andrew

Rank and organization: First Lieutenant, Company H, 30th U. S. Colored Troops.
Place and date: At the mine, Petersburg Va., 30 July 1864.
Entered service at: Otsego County, N. Y.
Born: 12 February 1840, Scotland.
Date of Issue: 17 October 1892.
Citation: One of the first to enter the enemy's works, where, after his colonel, major, and one-third the company officers had fallen, he gallantly assisted in rallying and saving the remnant of the command.

Day, Charles

Rank and organization: Private, Company K, 210th Penn Infantry
Place and date: Hatcher's Run, Va. 6 February 1865
Entered Service at: Lycoming County, Pa.
Born: Otsego County, N. Y.
Date of Issue: 20 July 1897
Citation: Seized the colors of another regiment of the brigade, the regiment having been thrown into confusion and the color bearer killed, and bore said colors throughout the remainder of the engagement.

Hawthorne, Harris S.

Rank and Organization: Corporal, Company F, 121st New York Infantry.
Place and date: At Sailors Creek, Va. 6 April 1865.
Entered service at: Otsego, N. Y.

Born: 1832, Salem, N. Y.
Date of Issue: 29 December 1894.
Citation: Captured the Confederate Gen. G. W. Custis Lee.

Kenyon, John S.

Rank and organization: Sergeant, Company D, 3d New York Cavalry.
Place and date: At Trenton, N. C., 15 May 1862.
Entered Service at: Schenevus, N. Y.
Born: 5 May 1843, Grosvenors, Schoharie County, N. Y.
Date of Issue: 28 September 1897.
Citation: Voluntarily left a retiring column, returned in face of the enemy's fire, helped a wounded man upon a horse, and so enable him to escape capture or death.

Mangam, Richard Christopher

Rank and organization: Private, Company H, 148th New York Infantry
Place and date: Hatcher's Run, Va., 2 April 1865
Entered Service at:
Born: 21 December 1841, Ireland
Date of Issue: 21 September 1888
Citation: For extraordinary heroism on 2 April 1865 while serving with Company H., 148 New York Infantry, in action at Hatcher's Run Virginia, for capture of flag of 8th Mississippi Infantry (Confederate State of America).
Death and burial: 18 November 1893, Worcester, N. Y.

Weeks, John H.

Rank and organization: Private, Company H, 152nd New York Infantry
Place and date: At Spotsylvania, Va., 12 May 1864
Entered Service at: Hartwick Seminary, N. Y.
Born: 15 March 1845, Hampton, Conn.
Date of Issue:
Citation: Capture of flag and color bearer using an empty cocked rifle while out numbered five or six to one.

BIBLIOGRAPHY

Arnold, Edwin O. *Letter to Friend Will.* August 30, 1863. Collection of Virginia Schoradt, New Lisbon Town Historian.

Baker, Harvey. [Compiled by Greater Oneonta Historical Society.] *Oneonta in Olden Times and Bits of Oneonta History: An Interesting Series of Articles by Harvey Baker, Published in the Oneonta Herald During the Years 1892-1893.* Square Circle Press. Voorheesville, 2010

Brophy, Marion. *The Town of Otsego: Home Front, 1861-1865, Compiled from The Freeman's Journal and Otsego Town Records.*

Chapin, William H. *Letter to Charlotte Chapin.* February 27, 1863 and April 16, 1863. Collection of Virginia Schoradt, New Lisbon Town Historian.

The Cherry Valley Gazette, Cherry Valley, N. Y.

Cherry Valley Historical Association, Cherry Valley, N. Y. Civil War File.

Chisholm, Andrew. *Letter to his sister, Mrs. Peleg Cornell.* October 4, 1862, October 21, 1862 and November 16, 1862. Collection of the Town of Burlington Historical Association.

The Daily Star, Oneonta, N. Y.

Daniels, John N. "Andersonville Prison in 1864." Printed in *The Morris Chronicle*, July 6, 1904. Morris, N. Y.

Fairchild, L. D. *Letter to his wife.* April 20, 1864 and November 20, 1864. Collection of the Town of Exeter Historical Society.

Fenton, Nathaniel. *Letters to his Almira, his wife.* Collection of Duane Bliss

The Freeman's Journal, Cooperstown, N. Y.

Greiner, James M. *Subdued by the Sword: A Line Officer in the 121st New York Volunteers*. State University of New York Press. Albany, 2003.

Hardaway, Cyrus J. *Letters to his mother*. Collection of William and Nancy Beardslee.

Mather, Andrew Adrian. *Diary*. Special Collections, The New York State Historical Association, Cooperstown, N. Y.

Myrick, Amassa Cook. *Civil War Letters to his Father*. Transcription by Larry Kading with help from Douglas McKee. The Local Collection of the Gilbertsville Free Library, Gilbertsville, N. Y.

The New York State Historical Association, Cooperstown, N. Y. Special Collections.

The Otsego Republican. Cooperstown, N. Y.

"War Reminiscences." Printed in *The Otsego Republican*. Delevan Bates. November 15, 1895 and January 31, 1896.

Paine, Lansing B. *Diary*. Copy from the collection of Virginia Schoradt, New Lisbon Town Historian.

Paine, Lansing B. *Letter to his parents*. May 4, 1863. *Letter to his sister Fan*. December 24, 1863. Collection of Virginia Schoradt, New Lisbon Town Historian.

Smith, Thomas. *Letters to L. W. Rathbun*. April 12, 1863 (?) and November 15, 1864. Collection of Robert Consigli.

Wendell, C. *The Third Annual Report of the Bureau of Military Statistics of the State of New York*. Albany, 1866.

Town of Exeter Historical Society, Schuyler Lake, N. Y.

Walton, Ann. *Life and Deeds of Seth Flint*. Barton-Butler Graphics. Cooperstown, 2002.

Dennis A. Dewy, "The Nineteen Soldiers of Plainfield." Printed in *The West Winfield Gazette*, March 6, 1914.

Wood, Henry Hilton. *Experiences and Activities of a Lifetime*. Privately Printed. Long Beach, 1934.

INDEX OF AUTHORS

Anonymous Poet (V. P), 123
Arnold, Edwin O., 85
Baker, Harvey, 45, 46
Ballard, John W., 69
Bates, Delevan, 72, 83, 84, 94, 120
Bureau of Military Statistics, State of New York, 118
Bryant, Lewis M., 109
Chapin, William H., 70, 73
The Cherry Valley Gazette, 10, 12, 14, 15, 26, 56
Chisholm, Andrew, 58, 62, 64
Connoford, James, 117
Consigli, Robert, 126
The Daily Star, 123
Daniels, John N., 106
Davidson, Robert B., 101
Devoe, Charles W., 42, 47
Doubleday, Abner, 11
Fairchild, L. D., 91, 104
Fenton, Nathaniel, 87
The Freeman's Journal, 8, 9, 16-23, 30, 32, 33, 69, 95, 96, 102, 103, 105, 110
French, Samuel D., 61, 95
Gordon, S., 106
Gould, Charles H., 98, 99

Hardaway, Cyrus J., 27, 40, 41, 43, 48, 50, 65, 82, 116
Harkin, John, 28
Hetherington, John E., 44, 98
Keith, Elijah, 39, 68, 80, 84, 97
Kidder, John S., 58, 66, 77, 79, 114
Mather, Andrew Adrian, 54, 70, 80, 84
Myrick, Amasa Cook, 36, 52, 57, 60, 67, 78, 81, 86, 90, 92, 115
Otsego, Town of, 94
The Otsego Republican, 31
Paine, Lansing B., 75, 88, 92, 116
Phinney, John, 37, 38
Rider, J. Lafayette, 18
Smith, Thomas, 73, 103
Snow, George, 38
Tyler, John K., 1
Weldon, Thomas F., 29, 53, 71
West, Charles B., 111
The West Winfield Gazette, 120
Winslow, Lester, 51
Wood, Henry Hilton, 30, 57, 66, 74
Wright, John, 89, 92, 102
Young, John W., 55

www.ingramcontent.com/pod-product-compliance
Lightning Source LLC
Chambersburg PA
CBHW071723090426
42738CB00009B/1860